RADIO CONTROL
PRIMER

RADIO CONTROL PRIMER

DAVID BODDINGTON

An introduction to radio control
of powered model aircraft

ARGUS BOOKS LIMITED

ARGUS BOOKS LTD.
Model and Allied Publications
Wolsey House
Wolsey Road,
Hemel Hempstead,
Herts HP2 4SS,
England

First published 1974
Second Impression 1975
Third Impression 1976
Fourth Impression 1977

Revised Edition 1981
Second Impression 1983

ISBN 0 85242 378 0

Printed by M & A Thomson Litho, East Kilbride

CONTENTS

CHAPTER ONE

THE CHALLENGE OF RADIO CONTROL

THE FANTASTIC growth rate of the hobby of radio control model aircraft over recent years has amazed everyone, even the people already connected with the hobby. For those modellers who have been happily pursuing radio controlled modelling for some years it has come as a surprise that their colleagues have at last awakened to the fulfilment of participating in 'his' hobby. Yet, the committed of us should not be surprised at this active interest in a hobby, or sport, that offers so much to the participant — it is only surprising that it has taken so long to get the message across to the unconverted.

How many pastimes can offer the benefits and interests of model aircraft, particularly radio controlled model aircraft? It can cover a complete spectrum of interests from the artistic aspirations of designing your own radio control model aircraft 'dream ship' to the tense excitement of taking part in a national or international competition. It covers both indoor and outdoor activities but leaves the choice of depth of involvement in the hobby to the individual. You may wish to start from 'square one' and construct a model from a plan, perhaps your own, fit in the radio equipment and engine and learn to fly it with a minimum of assistance from anyone else or, you may prefer to go to a shop and purchase a completed model, 'off the peg' so to speak, and concentrate on the pleasures of flying only. To the modeller, the thought of buying a ready to fly model may be close to sacrilege but, a golfer is not expected to make his own clubs and golf balls — so why should a modeller have to build his own model? I think it is true that the more you put into a hobby, or sport, the more you will get out of it and, the enthusiast that goes through the A-Z process of designing, building and flying, will probably obtain the maximum satisfaction. However, it is better to have experienced just some of the pleasures of the radio control model aircraft hobby than to have missed them entirely. In this book it is not intended to cover every aspect of the hobby, more comprehensive books are available, but to cover the basic explanations and to guide you through the initial problems of constructing and flying a radio controlled model. Having met the initial challenge, and tasted the excitement and enjoyment of this unique hobby, there is little doubt that you will want to explore some of the many branches of building and flying.

Radio control explained

Radio control, stated in its simplest form, is the remote control of, in this case, a model aircraft. How the remote control operates is, in many respects, of secondary importance and we do not have to be electronic geniuses to be able to install the equipment or learn how to operate it. A simple, non technical, explanation of the sequence of operation is given in chapter three but it

In the uncovered state the "Tinker" illustrates the simple construction used. See pages 8/9 for plan.

is probably of more interest to the novice to know what we can perform with the radio control equipment, rather than to know precisely the function of the many sophisticated electronic components used on modern outfits.

R/C (the normal abbreviation for radio control, both for the written word and speech) models vary from the simplest small models, fitted with non proportional rudder only control, to exact replicas of four engined bombers capable of retracting their undercarriages and dropping dummy bombs. A slow training model may fly at a speed of only fifteen to twenty miles per hour whereas a radio controlled pylon race model may well be travelling at over one hundred and fifty miles per hour; and calling for the absolute in skill and judgment of the pilot in flying the model around the prescribed course at low level. R/C aerobatic models are designed to be capable of performing all of the accepted aerobatics performed by full size aircraft — and a few additional ones too! The functions of the R/C equipment can just as easily be employed to operate the control of a model helicopter, although it is far from easy to fly these models, or a miniature sailplane — capable of soaring for hours, without benefit of an engine, but merely relying on lift provided by hills or thermals. It is immaterial whether you progress to being proficient in competition flying or prefer to stay as a 'sports' flier, without specialising in any particular aspect, the challenge and rewards will always be there. The man who thinks that he is bored because he has 'done everything' in R/C flying, or for that matter in most other sports and hobbies, is suffering from a delusion. The boredom is in himself and not in the hobby — that can provide more than a lifetime of interest.

Understanding flight

One of the problems created by the enormous influx of radio control modellers is the lack of basic knowledge they have on the understanding of how a model flies and, frequently, the lack of written information available for him to digest this information. Until recently many modellers joining the R/C fliers had come through the ranks of free flight or control line modellers. In this way these aeromodellers had a reasonable knowledge of aerodynamics, and knew how to trim a model to fly correctly. Their knowledge spread to the effects of control surfaces, wing loadings, centres of gravity, and the other basic information necessary to understand why a model flies — or doesn't. Unfortunately, the contemporary newcomer to the R/C hobby has not had the benefit of the grounding received in the other aspects of aeromodelling and he is in danger of starting flying before he is able to find sufficient answers to problems he may encounter. It is most important that the prospective R/C pilot should learn the basic theory of how a model flies, and how the controls affect the model, before taking that first step towards his first solo. It is the intention, in this book, to give you not only this basic theoretical information, but to take you, step by step, through choosing the radio equipment, building the model, installing the equipment and learning to fly. Let me make it absolutely clear at this stage that there is no foolproof system that will guarantee success. The aim will be to get you airborne with as little risk as possible, which does not mean that you may not get failures. It is only possible to 'instruct' you to a certain degree and from the point at which the model is in the air, regardless of the quality of the radio control equipment or suitability of the model, it will depend entirely on the person at the transmitter. No amount of written descriptions of what to avoid can prevent an inexperienced modeller occasionally giving the wrong control or 'freezing' on the controls. You must be prepared to damage or 'write off' at least one model, and perhaps more; if you are not prepared to make this sort of sacrifice, then it is probably better not to start the hobby. I have met very few 'natural' pilots (in fact, only one that I can recall) where the control of the model, orientation and general 'feel' of flying seems to come automatically.

When you see the local experienced club model pilot doing every conceivable manoeuvre with his aerobatic model, it all looks so easy — it is not! The only way you will achieve this standard is by practice and still more practice in all sorts of weather conditions, with a variety of models and, inevitably, a number of disappointments and setbacks. The weak will succumb, but the stronger ones will carry on to enjoy one of the most rewarding of hobbies.

CHAPTER TWO

REQUIREMENTS FOR FLIGHT

ONE OF THE biggest problems in writing a book for the beginners is to decide on how much basic detail to go into. Should one describe how balsa is grown, what a transmitter is, what effect wind shear has on a model coming in to land? Perhaps the basic knowledge necessary to the prospective R/C flier, and one that is often overlooked, is that of simple aero-dynamics or, what makes an aeroplane fly. The understanding of the principles of flight are important in understanding also what happens to a model during the various stages of its flight. When we are unfortunate enough to crash a model through a flying error it is important to know why it crashed, so that we can avoid making the same error again. It is not intended to pursue detailed aerodynamics for designing models, etc., but sufficient to understand why an aeroplane flies and what effect control surfaces have.

Let us first consider how an aeroplane stays up in the air. Although it seems to be the general view of mothers and wives that an aeroplane is kept in the air by the action of the propellor or, in the case of a jet, by being pushed upwards and forwards by the thrust of the jet engine, it is, of course, the

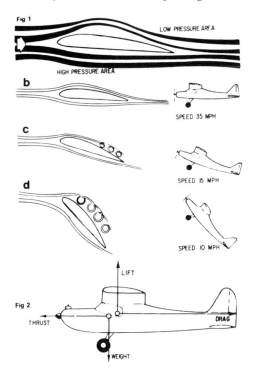

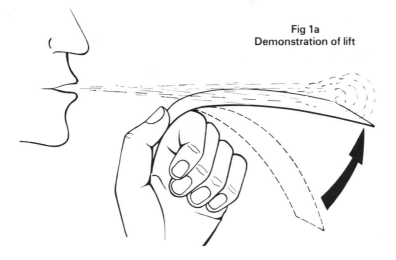

Fig 1a
Demonstration of lift

wings that create the lift to suspend the aircraft. Now, if we look at the side view of the plan of the model in *Fig 1* we can see that the wing is set at a slight angle, with the leading edge slightly higher than the trailing. When the model is being propelled forward in straight and level flight the air, when it reaches the leading edge of the wing, has to divide, some passing over the top of the wing and some underneath. The air passing beneath the wing is forced downwards, owing to the angle of incidence, and because it is now in an area of relatively high pressure, tends to push the wing upwards. Over the top of the wing there is, because of the angle of incidence and the camber of the upper wing surface, an increase in the speed of the air flow, causing an area of relatively low pressure, thus sucking the wing upwards. The combination of the area of high pressure pushing upwards and the low pressure over the wing sucking it upwards are together known as a lift. About two-thirds of the wing's total lift is created by the top surface of the wing and one-third from the airflow over the lower surface.

The lift created on the top surface can easily be demonstrated by holding a piece of note paper by one edge and blowing along the surface, notice how the paper rises. *(See Fig. 1a)*.

Lift is directly related to the speed of the model, and it therefore follows that if a model slows down too much there will be insufficient lift created to allow a model to fly — a most important point to remember during the launching or take-off and landing. *Fig. 1* shows the airflow over the aerofoil (wing) section in normal conditions and in b, c and d the airflow through straight and level flight, through a climbing angle and reduction in speed, until there is a break-up of the airflow over the wing. When the break-up of the airflow is reached, the model is said to be stalled, and control cannot be attained until the model is dived and flying speed built up.

Having seen how the model stays up, we can now consider the disposition

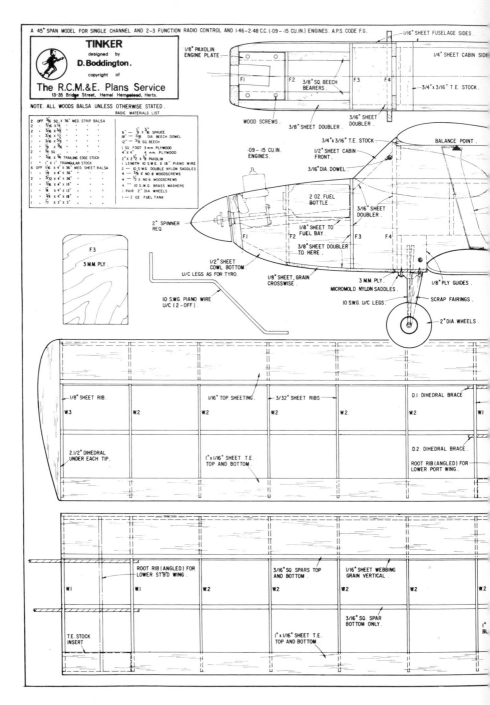

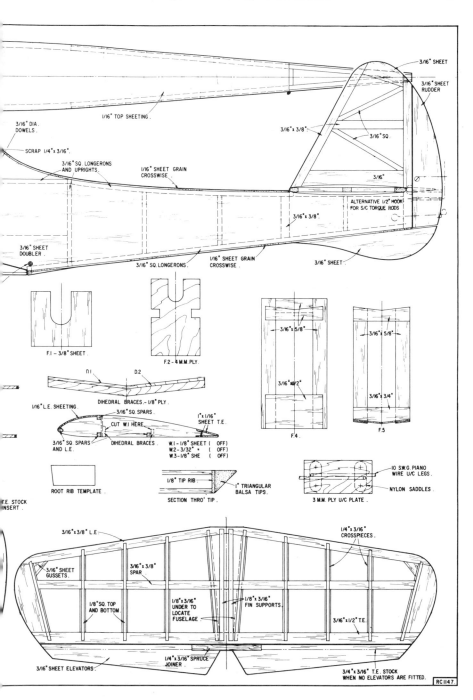

of other forces acting in flight, as shown in *Fig. 2*. Thrust is provided by the
engine 'pulling' the model forwards. The speed of the model is governed by
the power of the engine, the attitude to the ground, i.e., climbing or diving,
and the drag from the model; when the thrust of the engine is exactly
balanced by the drag of the model, the model will cease to accelerate. Various
types of drag are involved when the model is flying but, at this time, we will
just consider it as resistance to air. The lift must, as stated before, counteract
the weight of the model and because lift has to be increased by an increase of
speed, it is important to keep our model as light as possible. A heavy model
has to fly faster to stay in the air, and therefore landing and launch speeds
are higher — even the slow landing speeds can seem too fast for a beginner!
Notice that the thrust line and line of drag are not in line with one another,
thus causing a climbing effect unless counteracted. Although the line of
weight (acting through the centre of gravity) is offset compared to the line
of lift, to counteract this climbing effect it is often also necessary to change
the line by introducing engine down-thrust.

Having considered the forces acting upon our model, we will now take a
look at the axes through which a model can turn. *(Fig 3.)*

The diagrams are reasonably self explanatory and it is sufficient to say that
the control surfaces move the aircraft by creating more lift, as shown in *Fig.
4*. For the purpose of our training model we shall be considering the rudder
as a method of turning. This does not mean, however, that all our turns,
using rudder, will be flat yawing turns; as the yaw occurs the wing on the
outside of the turn creates more lift (and vice-versa for the inboard wing),
thus causing the outside wing to rise, and the model banks in the direction of
the turn. Note that when the model is in a steeply banked turn, the elevator in
effect becomes the rudder, or turning, action and, to a lesser degree, the

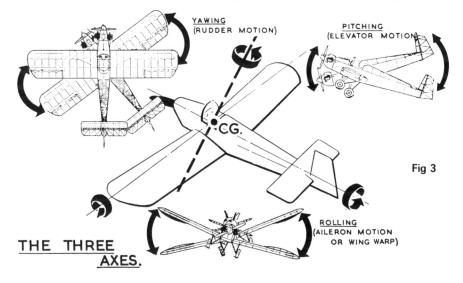

YAWING
(RUDDER MOTION)

PITCHING
(ELEVATOR MOTION)

.CG.

Fig 3

ROLLING
(AILERON MOTION
OR WING WARP)

THE THREE
AXES.

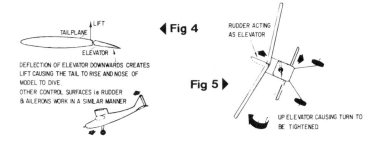

rudder becomes the elevator. *(See Fig. 5)*. This knowledge is important when we are trying to recover from a spiral dive, in these circumstances the application of up elevator will aggravate the condition and not improve it.

Ailerons give, when combined with elevator, smoother turns than achieved with rudder; less tendency for the nose to drop during the turn, and better axial rolls.

Ailerons may not be so effective when the model is at lower speeds, such as on the landing approach, when rudder may be used for correction of the direction of the model. For correction in direction during the take off run of a model, the ailerons are of no value as we need to yaw the model, (the model still being ground based) and not bank the model as required in flight. All competition aerobatic, and most scale and pylon racing, models feature ailerons in addition to rudder control and the only disadvantage to the beginner is the relative complexity of fitting the ailerons and linkages. I would always recommend incorporating ailerons to a second R/C model (in place of rudder if only two or three function radio is being used) as it increases the scope of flying considerably.

There we have a very potted version of basic aerodynamic principles. I have missed quite a lot of important information and over-simplified the science of aerodynamics but I consider it is more important for a few basic facts, relevant to initial flights, to be properly learnt rather than a whole lot of information that cannot be digested.

Aerodynamics is very much a subject on its own and should you find it of interest by all means carry out some research at your local library. Another Argus title, Model Aircraft Aerodynamics, price £9.95, is an excellent definitive work for further reading. Be warned though! If you get too involved there may well appear so many factors to consider, so many variables to calculate, so many reasons why a particular model should not or will not fly that you will probably never even get as far as the flying field.

CHAPTER THREE

THE RADIO CONTROL EQUIPMENT

RADIO CONTROL is, as stated in chapter one, a method of remotely controlling a model aircraft by operating the model's control surfaces and engine. Regardless of the simplicity (i.e. single function control operating rudder only) or the complexity (up to eight functions have been incorporated) of the radio control system the equipment comprises two parts.

1. **Ground Equipment**   — The Transmitter
2. **The Airborne System**   — Consistency of the receiver, decoder and the control actuating mechanisms (servos) and batteries.

To take the explanation to its next logical step would entail differentiating between single channel, pulse proportional and 'full' proportional control (sub dividing the latter into Digital and Analogue designs). In a book of this type, with limited technical information, I consider it is more important to discuss the problems of the types of equipment to purchase rather than spend time explaining the electronic methods of achieving the desired object. Sufficient to say that the hand held transmitter emits pulsed radio signals that are projected to the airborne receiver. The receiver collects, or picks up, these

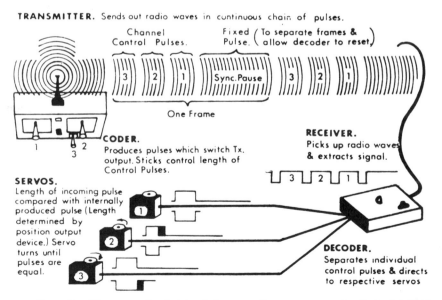

Opposite: Diagrammatic sketch of the operation sequence of a three function radio control outfit as well illustrated in the MacGregor instruction booklet.

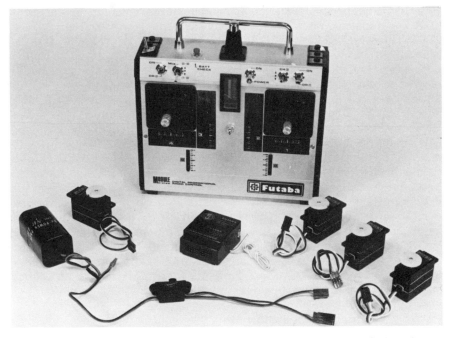

Modern sophisticated proportional outfits often feature "plug-in" modules on the transmitter for frequency changing. Also featured on the seven function transmitter are such "luxuries" as rate switches, mixers and roll buttons. None of these features are essential for the sports flyer but are useful additions for the experienced aerobatic competitor.

signals and passes them on to the decoder which, as its name suggests, separates the signals into their separate functions.

The final link in the system is the servo, the pulsed signals are passed to the servo where they are amplified and fed to the servo motor. The duration of the pulses dictates the direction of travel of the servo motor and thence, through gearing, to the output arm or disc.

Very precise frequency control is necessary for our radio control equipment as we are only allocated narrow wave bands by the Home Office for the purposes of operating our equipment. To be able to operate more than one model at a time, therefore, the allocated wave bands are divided into a number of 'spot' frequencies, identified by colours and numbers for ease of recognition. Appropriate pennants are fixed to the transmitters so that it is possible, at a glance, to check the frequencies of any transmitter.

The first frequency allocation for modellers was on the 27 MHz band and was arranged, with 50Kcs spacing, into the following 'spot' frequencies:–

Brown	26.995	**Yellow**	27.145
Red	27.045	**Green**	27.195
Orange	27.095	**Blue**	27.245 Mhz

With an increase in modelling activity, and an improvement in the standards of R/C equipment, intermediate frequencies (splits) were introduced, i.e. 27.020 (Brown/Red) 27.070 (Red/Orange) etc. Apart from a general overcrowding of the 11 spot frequencies, boat and car modellers having to use the same allocation, all was well until the advent of illegal C.B. (Citizens Band) radio. The imported CB sets often used frequencies identical, or very close to, the spot frequencies used by the modellers, with the obvious risk of interference being caused to the receivers fitted in the models. Models were in fact 'shot down' and the situation worsened until, after lengthy negotiations between the Society of Model Aeronautical Engineers (SMAE) together with the Model Hobby Trade Federation (MHTF) and the Home Office Radio Regulatory Department, the potentially dangerous position was alleviated by a complementary allocation on the 35 MHz band. This allocation, for R/C aircraft only, from 35.010 mHz to 35.200, is divided into 10Kcs spacing to make full use of the closer tolerance and reliable equipment now produced by manufacturers throughout the world. It is important when purchasing 35 MHz R/C equipment to ensure that it has the SMAE/MHTF approved sticker, whether it is of the A.M. (Amplitude Modulation) or FM (Frequency Modulated) type. The frequency pennants for 35 MHz have an orange background with the 'spot' frequency number superimposed on it, i.e.

35.010 MHz Pennant number 61
35.020 MHz Pennant Number 62

Two function low cost proportional equipment has become very popular for all forms of R/C modelling. A typical single action, function, transmitter stick assembly is shown on the right—note the trim lever.

Irvine/Sanwa FM Proportional equipment features a time alarm, with digital read out, on their 'Black Custom' outfit; useful for competition work and when engine operating time is critical i.e. multi engined models. Plug-in crystals allow rapid change of "spot" frequencies in the available band width.

35.030 MHz Pennant Number 63
and so on to:
35.200 MHz Pennant Number 80

The SMAE have also grouped the frequencies for various modelling aspects, the odd numbers for powered models and the even numbers for glider flying. However, individual clubs may have their own rules regarding the use of the allocated frequencies and it is wise to check with your local club or group to ascertain their arrangements. Indeed, it is sensible to visit the local flying field and ask the advice of members before purchasing any R/C equipment.

Coincidental with the allocation of the 35 MHz band for R/C model aircraft the government announced the legalising of C.B. for 40 'spots' between 27.600 and 28 MHz, i.e. *above* the 27 MHz frequencies used for model applications. Naturally, this did not mean that the many thousands of *illegal* C.B. sets were immediately thrown away but it does mean that the situation should gradually improve. Ironically the interest in C.B. has fallen dramatically since it has been legalised and the problems for modellers have reduced considerably. There had always been a tendency to overrate the effect of C.B. and many crashes have wrongly been attributed to interference when the reasons could have been more truthfully assigned to pilot error, poor installation or faulty equipment. In many parts of the country (Britain) it is still safe to fly on 27 MHz but, for peace of mind, it is logical to buy new equipment designed for operation on the 35 MHz band–or any new frequency bands that may be allocated to us by the government. No licence is now required for the operation of our equipment–not a totally desirable situation as it weakens our legal position when dealing with government bodies.

In addition to the VHF allocations there is also a spectrum on the higher frequency band around 459 Mhz. Different electronic design is required for operation at these higher frequencies (usually referred to as U.H.F.—ultra high frequency) and the transmitter is immediately recognisable by the short 'stub' aerial. Greater complexities of design and electronic circuitry result in higher initial costs of U.H.F. equipment (the matching of transmitter and receiver crystals is more critical) but, in all other respects, the equipment is equally suitable for R/C model aircraft flying—and less prone to interference. Although the range of U.H.F. equipment is normally limited to 'line of sight' this is unlikely to present problems to the R/C model flyer as the aircraft is, or should be, visible at all times.

35 MHz frequency R/C equipment is used in many European countries, 40 MHz and 72 MHz are also used in some countries. In countries where Citizens Band use is legalised on the 27 MHz band it is generally unsafe to operate R/C model aircraft on the recognised 27 MHz frequencies i.e. 26.995–27.245 MHz.

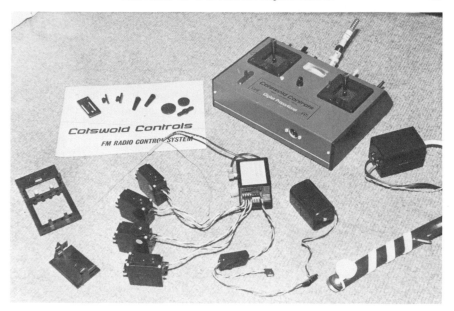

Cotswold Controls offer an alternative to the 27 and 35 MHz frequency R/C equipment by producing an outfit operating on the legalised 459 U.H.F. MHz band. Note the short aerials used on the receiver and transmitter, the latter incorporates a "Buddy-Box" training facility. More complex circuitry and higher specification crystals results in U.H.F. equipment costing more than the equivalent on the 27 and 35 MHz frequencies.

Many modellers seem to get confused about the 'range' of equipment i.e. the distance that the airborne equipment will operate satisfactorily from the transmitter. The range of our type of radio control equipment is, unlike domestic radio receivers and broadcasting transmitters, strictly limited. This limited airborne range, often in excess of one mile, works to our advantage; with virtually unlimited range only a limited number of modellers would be able to fly at a time in the **whole** country! The range of radio control equipment is rarely too small, except when caused by electronic faults, a model — even a large one — looks terrifyingly small at a distance of six hundred yards or so. Your eyes are likely to fail before the radio range does.

Selecting the equipment

Ask a half dozen 'experts' for advice on the type of radio control equipment the beginner should purchase and you will probably receive as many differing replies. Most modellers have preconceived ideas on the type and make of radio equipment the newcomer should invest in and opinions will be based on personal experiences; both good and bad experiences. It is difficult to give advice on the purchase of equipment until a number of facts are known i.e.

1. Am I confident that I shall sustain the interest in the hobby?
2. Can I afford to buy, outright or on H.P., the more expensive forms of equipment and still have enough money left over to purchase the model, engine and accessories — without causing financial disaster to the rest of the family?
3. Would I be content with the simplest forms of radio control and be happy to specialise in this limited field of control for model aircraft?

Transmitters come in all shapes and styles, some feature vinyl covered folded aluminium cases, others use injection moulded plastic. The Micron transmitter illustrated top right incorporates a three function stick assembly (ailerons, elevator and rudder—by a "twist" knob on top of the stick).

Most standard AM and FM receivers use "single deck" receivers with a single printed circuit board. Components, including integrated circuits, are closely spaced and the connector block for servo plugs is fitted at the end of the P.C. board.

In other words it is a question of dedication and costs. If your answer to number 3 is yes then you will probably be happy enough with two function equipment. Alternatively, an affirmative reply to questions 1 and 2 and you would be advised to purchase, right from the beginning, the radio equipment that you will eventually need. Normally that will be at least four function proportional equipment and possibly five, six or seven functions to cope with auxiliary controls in addition to the principal controls of rudder, elevator, ailerons and engine.

Before discussing the merits of purchasing a particular type of equipment it may be of interest to review briefly some of the earlier R/C equipment that is now virtually obsolete, except for historical interest.

Receivers featuring more complex circuitry, such as the Cotswold U.H.F. receiver shown here and S.S.M. (close tolerance AM equipment) may require a "double deck" construction to keep physical dimensions to a minimum.

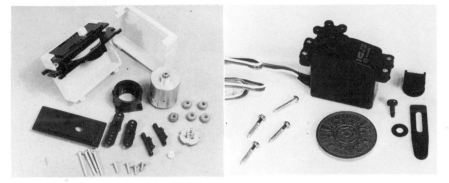

Servos come in Heavy duty, Standard, Miniature, and Sub Miniature sizes to suit all models from the smallest to large half scale models. Rotary outputs are most commonly used and are suitable for virtually all control linkages likely to be used in model aircraft.

Single Channel

The simplest form of R/C equipment giving, basically, non-proportional control of one function only–normally rudder. Rubber driven actuators or motorised servos were used and methods were devised to give rudimentary throttle control and a fixed position 'up' elevator by means of a 'quick blip' control. Many thousands of modellers learned to fly R/C models with single channel equipment; it had the virtues of being inexpensive and of teaching the operator to prepare and trim his model correctly before attempting to fly.

Pulse Proportional

In its simplest, rudder only, form this single channel system provides proportional control by allowing the constantly oscillating rudder to dwell fractionally longer on one side compared with the other. By using very small magnetic actuators and subminiature receivers operating off a three volt supply, or less, the total airborne pack weight can be as low as $2\frac{1}{2}$ ozs. Fully proportional R/C 'micro' systems are gradually coming down to comparable weights and this may result in the demise of the last of the commercial single channel systems–only Ace R/C in America now produce a pulse proportional system.

Pulse systems were also developed to incorporate elevator and throttle control, with distinct control limitations, but the advent of low cost fully proportional equipment ousted these 'Galloping Ghost' systems.

Reeds

Prior to modern multi proportional equipment the same functions were controlled by lever switches on the transmitter giving simple on/off movements of the control surfaces. Naturally, this made the flying of a multi-function model (fitted with rudder, elevator, aileron and engine control) considerably more difficult; the individual switches had to be 'pulsed' to obtain intermediate control positions.

Proportional

Proportional equipment, without doubt, is *the* most suitable type that will be purchased by at least ninety nine per cent of new modellers. The main consideration then becomes a question of how many functions, from one or one plus one (a fully proportional control plus a sequential non proportional function) to no less than eight functions. I firmly believe that, as previously implied, it is advisable to buy radio control equipment that will serve your needs for as long as you can forsee them. Two or three function equipment would be quite sufficient if your main interests are likely to be in gliders or sports models with limited performance. The vast majority of my proportional flying has been with two and three function systems and it has certainly caused no lack of enjoyment.

It is quite impossible, for various reasons, to give a full list of all of the manufacturers equipment and make recommendations of the 'best buy' type. Equipment is constantly changing, in price and specification, and it would be impossible to carry out comprehensive testing of all new outfits. Magazines, such as Radio Control Models and Electronics, will keep you up to date on the introduction of new equipment but even they are not able to review in 'depth' as most reviews are based on one example only. The difficulties of deciding which make to go for are considerable, reading the adverts will not help much — who ever advertised equipment as being sub-standard but, fortunately, most manufacturers produce a reasonable product.

This Sprengbrook Servo is available with rotary or linear outputs. Gear trains from the electric motor to the output shaft are constructed from brass or plastic, or a combination of both. High quality servos may also feature a ball raced output shaft.

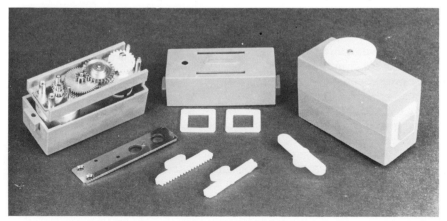

Sub miniature servos feature "watch making" precision and, despite their small physical size, offer sufficient power for normal sized powered model aircraft.

Manufacturers putting an inferior product onto the market tend not to stay in business too long whereas a long established firm is unlikely to be sending out rubbish year after year.

Developments of proportional equipment have been, and continue to be, rapid. Manufacturers, ever keen to improve their products and introduce new features, constantly update their equipment and the problems of selecting outfits become even more difficult. Not all of the new features are necessary, or even desirable; reliability remains the most important consideration for *all* modellers.

Without wishing to confuse the prospective purchaser by going into too much detail, these are some of the features you will see advertised:-

'Buddy Box' facility
Allows a teacher/student system to be used with a cable joining two transmitters (control being passed from the 'master' transmitter to the trainee at the press of a button). Highly recommended for learners, *provided* that similar equipment is possessed by other modellers in the club.

Rate switches
By operating a switch on the transmitter the maximum movement of the servo (usually elevator and aileron) is reduced. Not essential for training and sports models but can useful when moving on to aerobatic and scale designs for more precise control during normal flight.

Servo reversing
Moving a switch on the transmitter (fitted internally or externally) will change the direction of the servo rotation. Although this feature may seem to be desirable–it obviates the need for selecting the correct rotation of servo during installation–it is not without dangers. When more than one airborne pack is used with a common transmitter, a normal practice when a number of models have been built, there is the risk of forgetting to switch a servo to the correct rotation.

Mixer Controls
To couple two functions, e.g. rudder and ailerons or elevator and flaps. Desirable for some scale models and aerobatic types but not necessary for sports flying.

Dry cell equipment
Dry battery powered equipment is only suitable for the modeller with limited flying opportunities. If you hope to be out flying most weekends you should buy an outfit with rechargeable nickel cadmium cells, or with the facility to convert from dry cell to nicad operation without major modification.

It must be emphasised that the basic 4 or 5 function R/C outfits, without frills, are adequate for the vast majority of modellers. Only when you have advanced to more specialised models are you likely to *need* the more exotic auxiliary controls.

Probably one of the safest ways of making your decision is to visit a number of clubs, at their flying fields, in your local area and see what equipment they use and how satisfied they are with it. The chances are that there will be a predominance of one make of equipment, quite often produced by the nearest manufacturer and consequently handy for servicing and repairs. Despite the fact that nearly all equipment sold includes guarantees some are more comprehensive than others and it is vital that good servicing and repair facilities are available. To be able to take the equipment to the manufacturer, or their servicing agents, and explain the problems verbally to them, is far more satisfactory than having to rely on the postal service and a written report of the servicing required to be carried out.

Buying second hand equipment is one method of obtaining equipment more sophisticated than you may otherwise be able to afford. There are, of course, dangers in purchasing second hand equipment but providing you:-
 (a) Ensure the servicing and spares position is satisfactory.
 (b) Have a personal demonstration of the equipment, in flight, or know the past history of the outfit thoroughly.
 (c) Know that the equipment is capable of operating in accordance with present transmitting standards.
there is no reason why a second hand purchase should not prove to be a sound investment.

To summarise, we are looking for radio control equipment capable of:-
 (a) Working reliably through all normal conditions and circumstances thus giving the modeller confidence during his flying.
 (b) Be quickly serviced, and at a reasonable cost, for the knocks that are more than minor.
 (c) Be reasonably small and lightweight, but not at the expense of ruggedness. The equipment is likely to get somewhat rougher handling from the beginner than an experienced R/C modeller so subminiature servos and plugs may not be entirely suitable.

(d) Is easy to install and to transfer from one model to another.

I hope your choice of equipment turns out to be a good one but, if not, do let your retailer and the manufacturer know — it is no good simply bemoaning the troubles to your friends.

CHAPTER FOUR

CHOOSING THE MODEL

THERE HAS ALWAYS been a divergence of opinion between experienced modellers regarding the most suitable type of model for the purpose of ab initio training. One view is that it is better to jump straight in at the deep end and to build and fly a fastish aerobatic type model. This system may be acceptable when you have a tutor, preferably with a 'buddy box', who is prepared to spend a very long time in instructing. The advantage of a fast aerobatic model is that it can be flown in most weather conditions and is less affected by the wind, it has the disadvantage of being relatively unstable, requiring to be controlled at all times, and it **is** fast. Unless your reactions and thought processes are exceptional, I would suggest that you give this type of model a miss initially, except when nursed along by an extremely patient friend. At the opposite end of the scale is the ultra stable model which, with radio control fitted, is nearer to a guided free-flight model. This type of model has disadvantages; it is slow flying and may therefore be struggling a little to make headway against a wind, and it may have a greater tendency to over-climb at full power. There is no such thing as the ideal trainer to suit all persons and all conditions, but, in my opinion, the model with a considerable inherent stability is necessary and it should be capable of slow flight. Admittedly, choosing this type of model may restrict the number of days when the weather is suitable for you to fly but this seems a small price to pay compared with advantages. A stable model will often sort itself out of difficult positions that you have put it into, and, the fact that it is flying slowly,

David Boddington's "Pronto" can be built from the dimensioned plans on following pages, using full size rib section on pages 32/33. Suitable for .19 to .25 engines, it is very easy to make and has sprightly performance.

PRONTO

A 54" TRAINER FOR ·19 - ·25 ENGINES & 1 – 4 FUNCTION RADIO

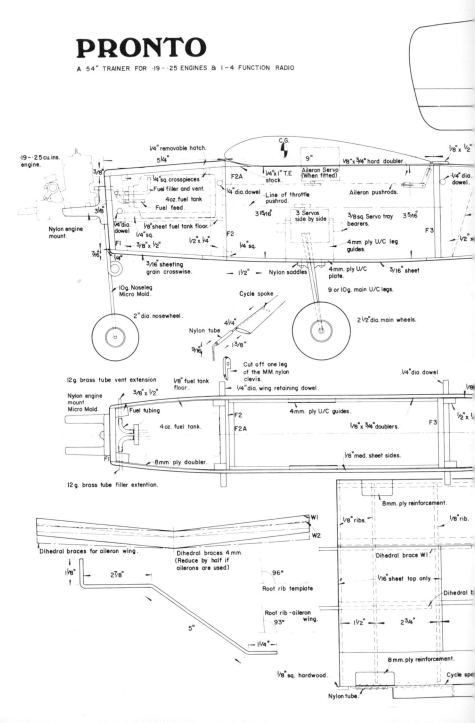

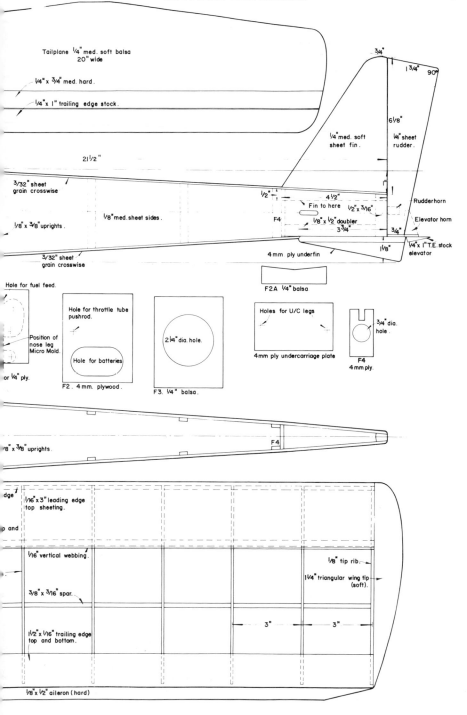

Tailplane ¼" med. soft balsa 20" wide

¼" x ¾" med. hard.

¼" x 1" trailing edge stock.

21½"

3/32" sheet grain crosswise

⅛" med. sheet sides.

⅛" x ⅜" uprights.

3/32" sheet grain crosswise

Hole for fuel feed.

Hole for throttle tube pushrod.

Position of nose leg Micro Mold.

Hole for batteries

or ¼" ply.

F2. 4 mm. plywood.

2 ¼" dia. hole.

F3. ¼" balsa.

Holes for U/C legs

4 mm ply undercarriage plate

¾" dia. hole.

F4 4 mm ply.

¾"

1 ¾"   90°

6⅛"

¼" med. soft sheet fin.

¼" sheet rudder.

1"

½"   4½"   ½" x 3/16"
            Fin to here
F4   ⅛" x ½" doubler
                3¾"   ¾"

4 mm ply underfin   ⅛"

Rudderhorn

Elevator horn

¼" x 1" T.E. stock elevator

F2A ¼" balsa

⅛" x ⅜" uprights.

F4

dge

1/16" x 3" leading edge top sheeting.

p and

1/16" vertical webbing.

3/8" x 3/16" spar.

1½" x 1/16" trailing edge top and bottom.

⅛" tip rib.

1¼" triangular wing tip (soft).

3"   3"

⅛" x ½" aileron (hard)

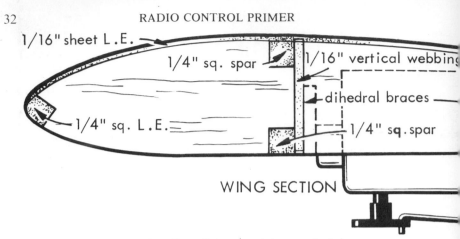

1/16" sheet L.E.

1/4" sq. spar

1/16" vertical webbing

1/4" sq. L.E.

dihedral braces

1/4" sq. spar

WING SECTION

'Pronto' wing section. Showing aileron linkage, and drawn actual size.

gives the trainee more time to think and then act. Rare indeed will be the trainee pilot who never gets disoriented, never gives a wrong signal, never watches the model, 'transfixed', and gives no control at all. The stable model is forgiving in character, most of us will find the operation of learning to fly will require a lot of patience and perseverance and we shall need a friend with those characteristics. For the 'loner' it is virtually essential.

'PRONTO'
For the purpose of discussing building, radio installations, control surfaces and flying a model we shall be using the 'Pronto' model as a basis. There are other designs equally as suitable for the job, but this was chosen in the

'Pronto'. A basic training model, designed with simplicity of building and flying as the foremost criterion. For .19 to .25 size engines.

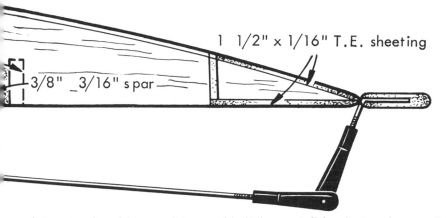

1 1/2" x 1/16" T.E. sheeting

3/8" _3/16" spar

interests of positive consistency of building and flying instructions, and the fact that it is simple to build and fly. There is sufficient information presented here to draw your own plans and to construct the 'Pronto'; alternatively you can purchase the full size plan or a comprehensive kit.

We discussed in Chapter 3 the different types of radio control but, in deference to the majority, we shall only consider in detail the installation and flying with two to four function proportional equipment. The **'Pronto'** is, in fact, suitable for all of the types of radio control system except for the single actuator 'galloping ghost' systems and pulse proportional rudder control, unless a double ended, high output magnetic actuator is used. Incidentally, when it comes to the choice of throttle positions (stick mode) on three or four function transmitters, I would not consider advising which to buy. It is mainly a matter of personal preference, many transmitters now have the facility to change the position of the throttle and elevator levers.

The design aim of the **'Pronto'** was to produce a simply constructed model, with good stability and flight characteristics, suitable for the complete novice to have a reasonable chance of success. Construction, although simple, must also produce a model of sufficient strength to stand up to most of the knocks that it is bound to get in the hands of the learner.

Before commencing construction, thoroughly familiarise yourself with the drawings, instructions and photographs and ensure that all stages of construction are fully understood. Cut out all sheet parts as this will save time at a later stage. For the majority of construction work a white P.V.A. glue, such as Evostik Resin or Bostik Carpentry adhesive, is recommended. Some modellers prefer to use an impact adhesive for large doubler areas, i.e. the ·8 mm ply nose doublers to the fuselage sides, but great care must be taken when placing the two surfaces together that they are in exactly the right position. The easiest way to achieve this is to place a piece of greaseproof or waxed paper between the two glued surfaces, after the adhesive has 'dried', and gradually withdraw the paper checking that the doubler is correctly

The fuselage side and doubler with former and upright positions marked on.

positioned before withdrawing too much of the paper. P.V.A. glue can be used for these doublers but remember that it will take a very long time for the glue to dry where the air cannot get to it; the side/doublers should be left, preferably lightly clamped together, at least overnight. Although P.V.A. glue does not dry as quickly as some other glues, i.e. balsa cement, this can be an advantage when tackling some of the slower jobs such as fixing the leading edge sheeting to the wings. In most cases the glue will be sufficiently dry to allow parts to be unpinned from the building board after about 3-4 hours.

Select the wood for the various parts of the model carefully and, in particular, try to get the quality of wood the same where they are 'paired' on the model, i.e. fuselage sides, left and right-hand wing spars, leading edge, fuselage longerons, etc. Keep the weight to a reasonable minimum but not by using the wrong strengths of balsa wood. It is not easy to specify exactly the right type of wood by labelling it medium or hard, etc.; if you are building the **'Pronto'** from the plan tell your supplier what the wood is needed for and, I have no doubt, he will assist you in choosing the right grade. A last plea before we start a detailed description of the construction, the finished model

Positioning the 8mm ply doubler on the 1/8th fuselage sides. The tracing paper is gradually pulled out, lining up the doubler at the same time.

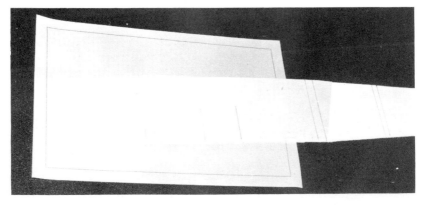

Fuselage side with doubler glued in position and ready for uprights etc.

will only be as 'true' as your building board, so do make sure it is absolutely flat and level. 'K' quality hardboard makes an excellent surface for building on, it takes pins just right, and if this is bonded to a flat surface, like marble, you have the perfect building board.

So, pin down the plan, rub over the building area with hard soap (to prevent the glue sticking to the plan) and off we go.

Fuselage

Mark on the ⅛ inch fuselage and ·8mm plywood doublers the position of all the formers, uprights, wing and undercarriage doublers etc. If you do this by putting the balsa under the plan, together with carbon paper, and pencilling on the plan, remember to put another layer of carbon paper (face up) under the plan. This will automatically mark on the reverse of the plan ready for making the opposite fuselage side. Glue to the sheet sides (one left and one right) ·8mm doublers, ⅛" x ⅜", ¼" x ½" and ⅜" x ½" uprights, ⅛" x ⅜" wing platform doublers etc.

Glue the 4mm plywood undercarriage leg positioners (unless a dural undercarriage is to be used) to each fuselage side noting that the left-hand

Uprights and doublers glued to fuselage side.

Formers F1, 2 and 3, glued to one side immediately prior to gluing in position the opposite side.

and right-hand positioners differ slightly. The plywood undercarriage plate can also be drilled at this stage, the staggered holes matching the slots in the positioners. Glue the ½" sq. fuel tank floor supports in position.

Drill F.1 to receive the nylon engine mount, fuel feed, throttle cable tube and nose leg saddle screws and screw the anchor nuts on the inside face for the engine mount bolts. Formers F1, 2, 3 and 4 can now be glued in position to both fuselage sides together with the full width ¼ in sq. cross member and fuel tank floor. Ensure that all formers are square and put the assembly aside until dry, then, bring together the rear ends sanding the stern blocks until they mate accurately. Check that both sides have an equal curvature and add the top and bottom balsa sheeting and plywood undercarriage plate. Fit the scrap trailing edge stock to the top of the wing seating area. Sand the whole of the fuselage thoroughly rounding off the corners especially around the nose area. The hatch to the fuel tank is removable and held by rubber bands over the dowels. Fit the undercarriage and engine mount after covering.

Wings
Wings are constructed in two sections and joined together with dihedral braces. Pin down a piece of 1½ in x 1/16 in trailing edge, and cut the hard lower spars to length and pin in position.

Glue ⅛in. and 3/32in. wing ribs in positions shown and check that all are

An alternative system of constructing the fuselage side, made up with all spacers, longerons and doublers in place. Two opposite sides required ... be careful not to build two left sides! This is on the Tyro Major, see Pages 56/57 for plan.

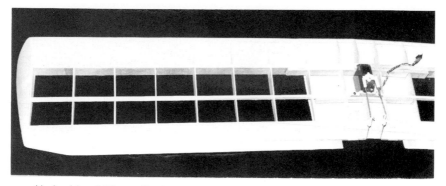

Underside of "Pronto" wing with aileron fitted.

vertical except for the root rib which should be angled from the root rib template. Glue the top spar in position. Fix the top trailing edge in position and glue the leading edge in place. When dry, remove from the plan and add 1/16in. sheet vertical webbing from top to lower spar. Add 1¼in. soft balsa tips and sand, together with the leading edge, to smooth contour as shown on the section drawing.

Construct the second opposite side panel in a similar manner. When both panels are set, cut slots with a razor saw in the first three root ribs to receive the dihedral braces. Check these for accurate fit and then glue into position on one wing panel. When dry, add the second wing panel to the projecting dihedral brace, glue thoroughly and pin down. Prop up the opposite wing tip to 5¼in. to obtain the correct dihedral angle. A lower dihedral may be used for aileron wings. Hold firmly in position until dry, pinning the two root ribs together. Add the centre section 1/16 sheeting to the top only. Sand completely and glue trailing edge and leading edge reinforcement in position.

Ailerons

For the ailerons to be effective it is necessary to reduce the dihedral by 50% and dihedral braces for the wing are shown. A total of 2¾in. for both wings is required. Although strip ailerons are shown on the plan there is no reason why you should not install inboard ailerons should you prefer them. These should be positioned in the last three of each wing panel and be approximately two inches wide.

Use a hard firm balsa for the strip ailerons and groove and drill carefully to receive the aileron torque rod. Reinforce the top and bottom of the aileron at the position of the hole with scrap ·8mm plywood. The torque rod is formed from a cycle spoke, as shown, note that the threaded end is raked forward so that the clevis 'horn' does not foul Former 3 during operation. Note also that a small piece of ⅛in. sq. hardboard is glued to the centre of the trailing edge of the wing to prevent the wing moving too far back and trapping the aileron pushrods. To fit the aileron servo it is necessary to cut away part of the two

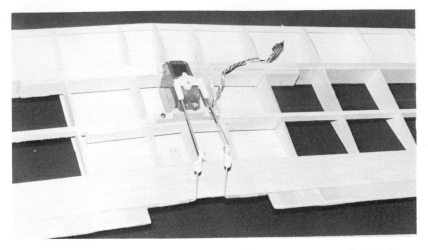

"Pronto" wing before covering but with the aileron servo temporarily fitted to check operation.

centre section ribs and also to install hardwood bearers for mounting the servo.

Tail surfaces
Use a light but firm grade of ¼in. sheet balsa for the tail surfaces although

The strip aileron linkage to the "Pronto" wing fitted temporarily before covering seen from another angle.

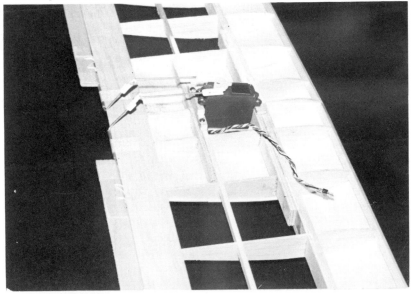

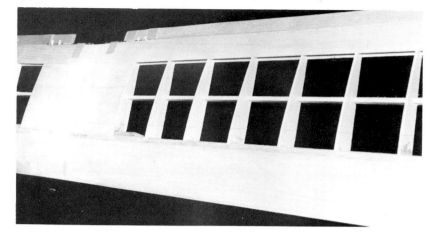

The centre section top sheeting is fitted to the wings after they have been joined.

the ¼in. x ¾in. for tailplane and the ¼in. x 1in. T.E. stock, used for the elevator should be of medium hard grade. Round off the leading edge of the tailplane and fin; the trailing edge of the elevator only requires lightly rounding off but the rudder should be tapered to about a sixteenth of an inch at the trailing edge. Hingeing surfaces will be rounded off or chamfered according to the type of hinge to be used.

The fin slots through the top fuselage sheeting into the former F4 and adjacent to the fuselage stern posts. Tail surfaces may be glued to the fuselage before or after covering, it is generally easier to cover them first but ensure that Kwik Cote or Solarfilm is cut away from the surfaces to be joined. It is essential that the areas actually contacting during the glueing

The wing panels are joined gluing the dihedral braces across the spars and using clothes pegs to butt the two centre section ribs together. In this case on Tyro Major.

should mate accurately and not rely on the glue to fill any gaps. It is also important to fix the tail surfaces squarely and true, check by eye **and** by measuring from a fixed reference point, i.e. from the centre of the fuselage at the wing position to tailplane tip. For the fin and rudder, measure from each tailplane tip to the top of the fin, equal lengths indicate that the fin is at ninety degrees to the tailplane.

Undercarriage

Do not try to bend the coil on the noseleg yourself unless you have the proper equipment to do it — it will simply be a waste of wire. Bending the main undercarriage legs, from 9g or 10g piano-wire, is easy providing you approach it correctly. Mark off the bending points with a felt pen and bind the area with Sellotape. Put the wire into a metal vice to the first mark and bend the long end, using a block of wood to push it over.

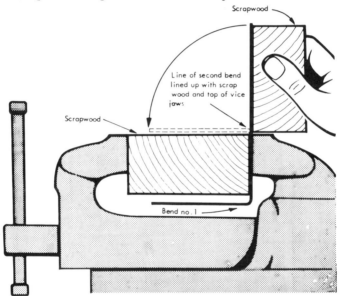

Continue to the next mark and bend again to the desired angle but now commence again from the opposite end so that the last bend does not entail attempting to bend a short length projecting from the vice. The nylon saddles, securing the main undercarriage legs, have a slot to take two widths of piano wire, if you cannot obtain special saddles single slot saddles can be filed out to increase the width. The undercarriage is not mandatory and if you expect to fly from a rough or long grass area you could well be better off removing the undercarriage entirely (if the undercarriage is removed after completion check the balance point again and add nose weight if necessary).

During construction try to bear in mind that the finished model will only fly well if it is built true, without twists and warps so do not be tempted to rush the building.

Parts List

1 sheet ¼" x 4" x 36" Med Soft
1 sheet 3/16" x 3" x 36" Med
4 sheets 1/8" x 4" x 36" Med Hard
3 sheets 3/32" x 4" x 36" Med
5 sheets 1/16" x 3" x 36" Med/s 3 Med
1 sheet 18" x 9" x .8mm Plywood
1 sheet 12" x 6" x 3mm Plywood
1 sheet 12" x 6" x 4mm Plywood
1 piece 3" x 4" x 5mm Plywood
1 length 3/8" x 3/8" x 6" Ramin Servobearers
1 length 1¼" x 1¼" x 18" Triangular
1 length 1" x ¼" x 36" T.E. Stock
6 lengths ¼" x ¼" x 36" Hard
2 lengths 3/16" x 3/8" x 36" Hard
1 length ¼" x ¾" x 36" M.H.
1 length ¼" x ½" x 36" Hard
1 length 1/8" x 3/8" x 36" Hard
1 length ½" x 3/8" x 9" Hard
1 length ¼" dia. Beech dowel x 18"
1 length ¼" dia. Ramin dowel for pushrods

Accessories

4oz Fuel Bottle
2 No 9 or 10g Double Saddles and 1 No 10g Saddle (Micro Mold)
1   Micro Mold N31 Nylon
        Engine Mount
1   Micro Mold N33A 10g.
        Nose Leg
4   4 b.a. Anchor Nuts
8   Small wood screws for anchor nuts
6   Self Tapping screws for nylon saddles
2   2½" dia. Wheels
1   2" dia. Wheels
6   Washers
2   9g. or 10g. main U/C legs
2   Nylon Horns
7   Nylon clevises
7   Clevis Spokes
1   3" length Nylon Tube
1   6" length plastic tube for Throttle Cable
3   Quick Keepers

Whether you follow the advice given in this book precisely i.e. you build a **'Pronto'** training model, or you build some other training model is not too important. It is important, though, not to get carried away and attempt to build a 'Spitfire', 'Lancaster', 'Gnat' or some other totally unsuitable design for your first attempt. Keep it simple!

CHAPTER FIVE

CONTROL SURFACES AND RADIO INSTALLATION

THE SUCCESS OF flying a radio control aircraft depends on the model being built accurately, the engine running reliably, the radio equipment operating faultlessly and the linkages, control surfaces and radio being installed satisfactorily. It is these last links in the chain that are often the weakest and particularly so for the trainee builder and flier. Try to approach the installation of the equipment and control surfaces with a logical and positive attitude, it is not something to be considered as additions to the model but an integral and vital part of the whole. Your common sense should tell you whether, for instance, a servo is safely mounted or an aileron linkage is free enough; if you are not satisfied in your own mind do not be tempted to leave it — correct the fault, it could save you many pounds and a lot of frustration.

Hinges
Regardless of how good and accurate your radio equipment is, and manufacturers are constantly aiming to improve the resolution of their equipment, the results can be nullified by the modeller making a poor job of the hinging of

Drilling the holes into elevator for a thread hinge. Note the foam rubber to protect the elevator during drilling.

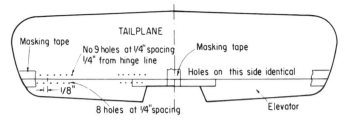

Drilling the tailplane and elevator for a sewn hinge.

the control surfaces and installation of the pushrods and control horns. The aims to achieve a good control surface hinge are:

(1) Freedom of movement.

(2) Close coupling of the control surface to the wing, fin or tailplane.

(3) Strength of the hinge.

Freedom of movement of the hinge action, is one of the most important considerations and described in practical terms, means that, without the pushrods being connected, the control surface should 'flop' from side to side under its own weight. Although modern proportional servos may have an output of 2½-3½ lbs. thrust this is no excuse whatsoever for taking the attitude that it does not matter if the control surface hinges are stiff because the servo power will overcome the stiffness. Certainly, the controls will still probably operate but this added load, together with the air loads on the control surfaces during flying, will be at the expense of greater battery drain and generally of accuracy too.

Sewing a thread hinge for an elevator.

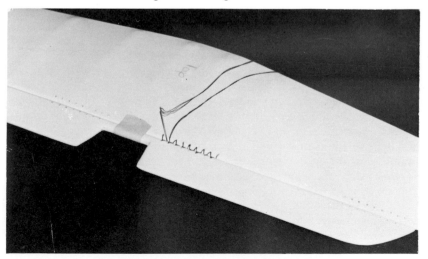

Thread hinge completed, with elevator horn close to hinge line.

One of the original forms of hinging control surfaces, and in many ways still one of the best, it the thread hinge. It gives a very free hinge, is simple to install and is certainly cheap. The disadvantages are that it looks rather more unsightly than some other methods, can be excessively sloppy unless correctly carried out and, if the wrong thread is used, insufficiently strong for prolonged periods of flying. Carried out with care and thoroughness however, it will give a very serviceable hinge. We will consider hinging the elevator, although the rudder hinging will be similar.

Using masking tape, join the elevator to the tailplane at the centre and the tips. Mark off, with ball point pen, positions of holes at ¼ in. centres, and about a ¼ in. out from the hinge lines as shown on the sketch. Note that the hole positions on the tailplane and elevator are staggered by ⅛ in.

Remove the masking tape and drill the holes with a fine drill, just large enough to take the needle to be used for sewing. When using a pillar drill for this operation, put a piece of rubber carpet underlay under the tailplane and elevator, during drilling to prevent damage to them. On no account omit the drilling of these holes, it may be possible to push a needle through the balsa without pre-drilling but it will almost certainly result in the balsa wood splitting along the grain between the holes. Fix the elevator back in position, this time using masking tape at the centre and one tip only. The most suitable forms of thread for hinging are Terylene (Keil Kraft sell cards of white Terylene thread) or nylon monofilament line of the type fishermen use (the finest line with a maximum breaking strain of 10 lbs. is perfectly adequate). The Terylene is probably easier to use and can be used double so, when threading the needle, loop it right through and tie the two ends

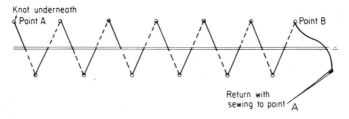

Method of sewing hinge.

together. Start sewing at the inboard hinge on the side without the masking tape. From the underside of the tailplane, push the needle through the first hole Point A, and pull the thread through the hinge line, this can be done by 'sliding' it down the gap from the tip, and push the needle up through the first hole in the elevator. Continue in this method until you reach the last hole Point B, in the tailplane and then back to the starting point thus completing the cross pattern of hinging.

Construct the other hinges in a similar manner, removing the masking tape at the tip when commencing the hinges on the opposite side. Leave the masking tape at the centre in position as this will be useful when installing the pushrods at the later stage. Put a dab of glue of fuel proofer over the holes to prevent ingress of fuel.

Moulded Hinges
Commercial hinges of various types are specially produced for model work and can provide a very neat installation and smooth operation. They do however, require accurate positioning and alignment. Because the material used for these hinges is not readily glued with conventional adhesive, holes are often left in the 'Leaf' of the hinge for the glue to penetrate and 'lock' the hinge in position. The two main types of moulded hinges are (1) the leaf and pin hinge and (2) Mylar hinge with 'thinned' hinge line.

The Mylar type hinge will never be as free in operation as the pinned or thread hinges but the resistance is not sufficiently great as to be detrimental to the radio equipment, providing that all other linkages are free in operation.

As stated previously, correct alignment of moulded hinges is absolutely vital and, therefore, marking and the cutting of the slots for the hinges are required for the elevator (two each side of the centre line) plus one pair for the rudder. Again we will consider installation of the hinges for the elevator. Mark the positions of the hinges on the elevator and tailplane making sure you mark a centre line along the edge of the elevator and tailplane. Cutting slots for the hinge halves must be carefully done to prevent cutting at an angle and slicing through to the surface. The use of a guide (⅛ in. x ½ in.) will assist here to make a slot parallel to the surface. It may be difficult to cut a slot of sufficient width with a knife and the slot must then be 'opened up' by using a jewellers flat file or a manicure sander. (The sort ladies use for filing down their nails). One common mistake modellers make is that, with pinned hinges, they tend to leave the circular part of the hinge projecting beyond the control surface. The result of this, with the hinge fixed, is a gap of about 1/16 in. between the elevator and tailplane. This is not only bad from the point of aerodynamic efficiency but may also cause the elevator to flutter during flight, putting unncessary strain on the hinges and servo. With hinges that require 'pegging' (the Micro Mold hinge N15 has a 'wedge' built in to prevent easy withdrawal) the hinges must be fitted before covering otherwise 'pegs' will show through the finished surface.

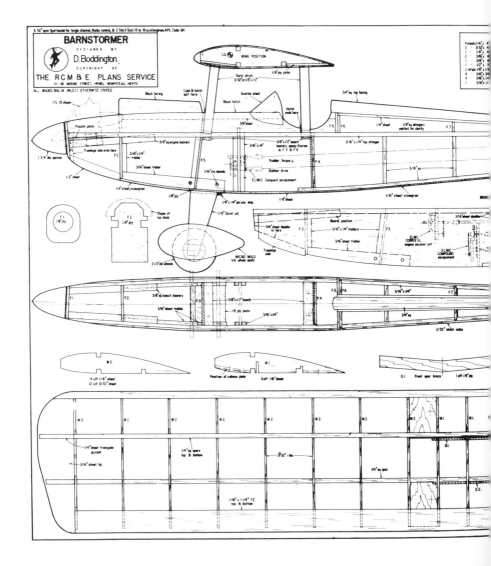

The model should be supported under the balance point for launch. This is the author's 52 inch. span Barnstormer, plans below.

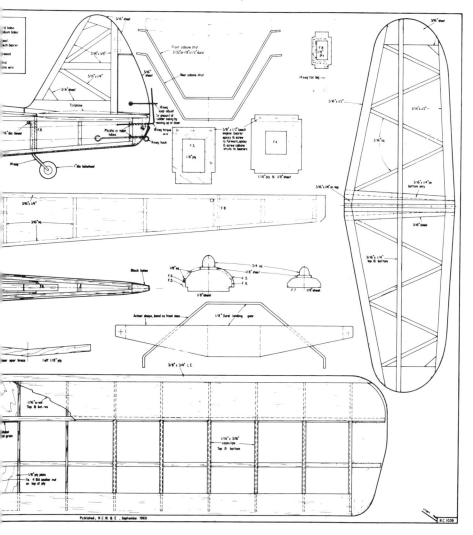

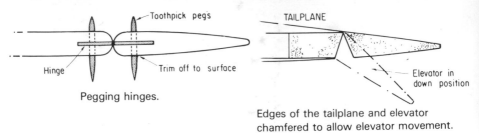

Pegging hinges.

Edges of the tailplane and elevator
chamfered to allow elevator movement.

When hinges are fitted after the model has been covered, ensure that no
epoxy glue gets onto the pivot part of the hinge. Either protect this part with
masking tape or smear the critical parts with Vaseline.

Mylar strip hinges

This method of hinging relies on the inherent toughness of relatively thin
Mylar sheet to act as the hinge. Compared with the moulded hinge the **Mylar**
strip is of constant thickness requiring a thinner slot to be cut in the elevator
and tailplane but possessing no gluing facility. Because we cannot glue the
hinge into position we must rely entirely on 'pegging' but this can be done
with steel domestic pins. The smaller diameter of these pins allows the hinges
to be fixed after covering the model and, when trimmed off with wire cutters,
does not mar the appearance of the model.

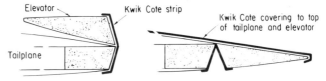

Method of forming a hinge.

Kwik Cote and Solarfilm hinges

These popular forms of plastic, self-adhesive, heat shrinking covering
materials can be adopted to form functional and free hinges. As these are
also produced at the same time as the covering operation there is also a
saving in time and money. Using Kwik Cote or Solarfilm means that the
hinge line, for ease of application, must be on the top or lower surface; for
appearance reasons it is normally the top surface of the ailerons or tailplane.
To obtain a sufficient degree of down elevator travel, the edges of the tailplane and elevator must be bevelled and for strength a double thickness of
the covering material is required at the hinge point, the sequence of covering
is shown here.

The underside of the tailplane and elevator are then covered as normal.
For the ailerons and rudder the same principle applies, using bevelled edges,
but it does mean that a 'Vee' joint will show on one side.

There are a number of other specialised hinges on the market but the ones
described here are the principal types. Do remember that, irrespective of the

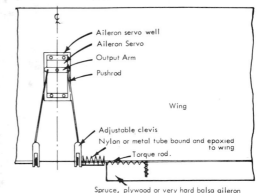

Fig. 1. Strip aileron linkage.

Fig. 2. Advanced trainer, such as the "Sky Rider" shown here, is the next step from the "Pronto." With a wing span of 63 inches the "Sky Rider" is suitable for 3/4 function radio and .40-.60 cu. ins. engine. Has strip ailerons.

type of hinge, it must have free movement. If you are not satisfied with the finished result it is cheaper to change it at this stage rather than wait until it causes the model to crash during flight tests.

Ailerons

There are two main types of ailerons (1) Strip ailerons and (2) Inset ailerons.

Strip ailerons, as used on the **'Pronto'** are the simplest form of aileron to build, and attach to the wing, and have proved, in competition aerobatics, to be equally efficient as the inset variety. When used with a torque rod connection to the aileron servo, the wing can be completed before the ailerons are attached, there being no internal linkages in the wing. For small models very hard balsa, plywood, or spruce strip may be used, rounded off on the leading and trailing edges *(Fig. 1 & 2)* but for larger models thicker sheet balsa or trailing edge stock must be used. One disadvantage with a torque rod connection to a strip aileron is the difficulty of using a top hinge, as frequently used when Solarfilm or Kwik Cote covering is employed. The reason

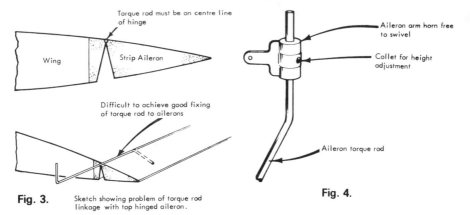

Fig. 3. Sketch showing problem of torque rod linkage with top hinged aileron.

Fig. 4.

for the problem is that the torque rod must always be in line with the hinge and this makes it difficult to obtain satisfactory fixing of the torque rod arm in the root of the strip aileron *(Fig. 3)*.

There are many commercially made strip aileron linkages available and, ideally, the aileron arm horns should be adjustable for height and free to swivel *(Fig. 4)*. The nylon or metal torque rod tube must be securely fixed to the wing trailing edge either by sewing and epoxying or by wrapping with glassfibre bandage and applying fibreglass resin. Clean and roughen the tube before fixing the tube to the trailing edge. Naturally, for this type of strip aileron connection to operate correctly the servo must rotate in the required direction, i.e. clockwise rotation when "left" is applied for a low or high wing model. Should all of the servos in your equipment operate in the same direction — and incorrect for strip ailerons — the direction of rotation of one servo will have to be changed, or an intermediate bellcrank used to reverse the movement.

Adjusting ailerons, to ensure they are true with the wing, is difficult and it is advisable to make a simple plywood template to check on both wing panels *(Fig. 5)*.

Fig. 5.

Inset ailerons

Inset ailerons, as the name suggests, are 'cut' into the wing in outboard section of the wings, in a similar manner to that employed by full size aircraft (see *Fig. 6*). Metal pushrods (16g. piano wire) together with nylon aileron cranks are normally used in built up balsa wood wings as this type of linkage is reasonably free from 'slop' and, properly installed, is smooth in operation

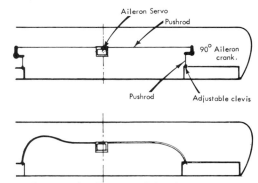

Fig. 6. Installation of inset aileron.

Fig. 7. Cable and tube installation.
Left panel shows the correct run.

without undue friction. An alternative, and often used in foam covered wings where a bell crank system can be difficult to install, is to use the Bowden cable type system *(Fig. 7)*. Stranded metal cable in nylon tube, nylon tube in a larger outer nylon tube or nylon rod in nylon tube may be used for this form of aileron linkage but the successful operation of the installation will depend on being able to route the tube through the wing without creating any sharp bends. It is essential that the tubing has described the full 90° arc before it exits the wing, to connect with the aileron horn, otherwise a side load will be transmitted to the aileron horn during operation. By virtue of the necessity for a reasonable clearance tolerance between the outer tube and the inner cable/tube/rod there is inevitably a degree of 'play' when this form of linkage is installed with a bend. On operation of the servo the inner cable will move first to the outer or inner curvature of the internal wall of the tube before transmitting the movement to the aileron horn *(Fig.8)*. A further disadvantage, when used on small wings, is the relative bulkiness of the adaptors used from the inner cable/tube/rod to the adjustable nylon clevis. With limited distances available, from the servo output to the edge of the servo well and from the aileron horn to the exit position in the wing, it may be a problem to fit in the adaptors and clevises. All tube/cable linkages should be checked periodically for freedom of movement as the ingress of oil or water can cause severe tightening in operation.

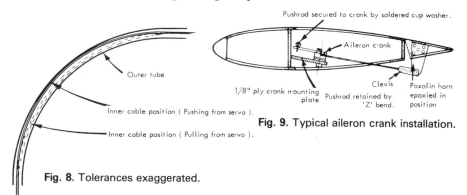

Fig. 9. Typical aileron crank installation.

Fig. 8. Tolerances exaggerated.

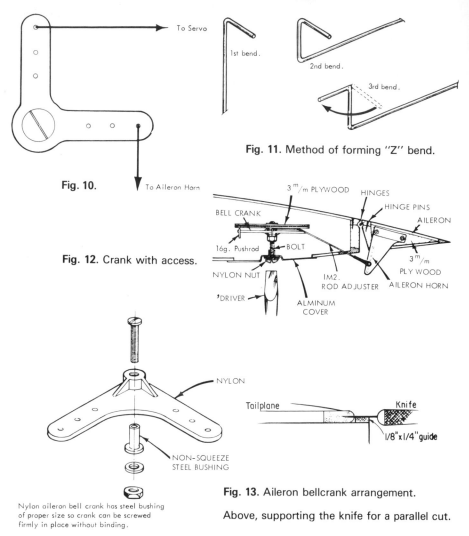

Fig. 10.   To Aileron Horn

Fig. 11. Method of forming "Z" bend.

Fig. 12. Crank with access.

Nylon aileron bell crank has steel bushing
of proper size so crank can be screwed
firmly in place without binding.

Fig. 13. Aileron bellcrank arrangement.

Above, supporting the knife for a parallel cut.

Inset strip ailerons

This contradiction in terms is really a combination of the two types of ailerons and is suitable for small models and fast models requiring only small movements i.e. Pylon racers. Note that with this form of installation the ailerons are fitted in the mid span position; with a fully outboard aileron the whip' on the torque rod would be too great.

Aileron crank installations

There are many commercially available aileron cranks, and although they vary in detail of design and manufacture they all work on the same principle of changing the direction of operation through approximately 90⁰. One added advantage of having a bell crank in the linkage, between the servo and the aileron horn, is that the extent of movement can be adjusted at this point. With linear servos it is not possible to vary the movement from the servo, and, if the full movement is transmitted to the aileron, to decrease the aileron movement to a reasonable degree may involve the use of an extra long aileron horn. By utilising the inner holes of the crank arm leading to the aileron horn the linear movement can be reduced *(Fig.10)*.

Naturally, before the linkage is installed in the wing the direction of servo rotation, or travel with a linear servo, must be ascertained and pushrod connections to the aileron cranks and aileron horns designed so that the transmitter operation and aileron movements agree, i.e. with the transmitter aileron stick to the left the left aileron is up. It is all too easy to connect ailerons incorrectly so do check carefully that they are working in the right sequence and also that as one aileron goes down the opposite aileron rises.

Aileron cranks are normally mounted on ⅛ in. (3 or 4 mm.) plywood plates glued between two wing ribs. Where ribs are at spacings that would cause flexing in the plywood mounting plate it is advisable to insert an additional half rib to reduce the spacing. Pushrods can be secured in position in the aileron crank either by bending the end through 90⁰, inserting through the crank and soldering with a cup washer or, by forming a 'Z' bend which is inserted through the crank before it is bolted to the plate. Methods of installing the aileron crank and forming the 'Z' bend are shown in *Fig.11* and in *Fig.12* an aileron crank installation with access for inspection and maintenance is also illustrated.

Aileron servo installation

The pushrod connection to the servo will vary according to the type of servo used, the linear servo being easier to link with, compared to the rotary output servo (Fig.14). Rotary servos can be connected in a number of ways, one of the original methods being shown in *Fig.15*. An alternative method, that avoids soldering the two pushrods together, is shown in *Fig.16* and this method is made even more simple with servos featuring a spline fitting for the output disc allowing a fully variable positioning of the disc.

Aileron servo mounting is made much easier by the use of a moulded nylon servo bracket but, when these are unavailable brackets can be made by

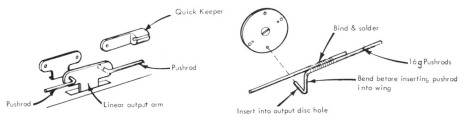

Fig. 14. Linear Servo connection.   **Fig. 15.** Rotary Servo connection.

cutting ⅜ in. - ½ in. wide sections from dural angle section (1 in. x 1 in. x ⅛ in.). Servos may also be secured by using double sided adhesive tape — servo mounting tape — but the bottom of the servo well, whether using plywood or balsa wood, must be finished to a smooth and well filled surface. Dope, balsa cement or epoxy may be used for this purpose.

Aileron horns

Again a wide variety of commercial aileron horns are obtainable or you can make your own from 1/16 in. thick paxolin or plastic laminates such as 'Formica' and 'Warerite'. With the thin paxolin type horns the horn should be epoxied securely between two hard balsawood or plywood aileron ribs and to ensure the epoxy grips well the top of the horn is drilled with a number of 3/32 in. dia. holes to allow the adhesive to penetrate. Standard rudder horns may be used for ailerons, in the case of strip aileron they are bolted right through the aileron and for the inset ailerons a plywood plate must be installed in the underside of the aileron. It will be noted that with the aileron horns installed as shown in *Figs. 11* and *17* the hinge line does not correspond with the horn/clevis pivot and this will inevitably involve a differential in aileron movement. Fortunately the differential works to our advantage in this instance as the down going aileron travels less distance than the up going aileron. The down going aileron provides additional lift but, if the movement is too great the additional lift is nullified by the extra drag caused by the aileron being deflected into the airflow. Should an equal movement, up and down, be required for the aileron the horn must be raked forward to coincide with the hinge line *(Fig. 18)*.

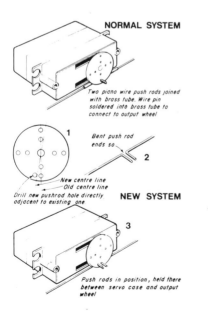

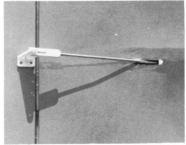

Above, aileron connection for strip aileron with bell crank linkage.

Left, **Fig. 16.**

Below, **Fig. 17.** Horn fining to strip aileron.

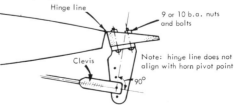

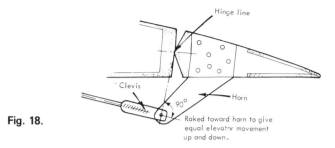

Fig. 18.

Aileron hinges
Methods of hinging ailerons are similar to those used for the rudder and elevator and the type of hinge used will determine whether a centre hinge or top hinge is used.

A final reminder to check thoroughly that the aileron installation is completely free in operation, and that all the cranks, horns and pushrods are secure, before the wings are finally covered.

Installation of radio equipment
It is not possible, because of the wide range of radio control equipment, to describe the installation of each and every piece of radio equipment manufactured. This instruction course will deal with general principles and basic forms of installation but more specifically related to modern forms of proportional equipment.

Planning the installation
In a previous chapter I have emphasised the need to keep the finished model as light as possible, consistent with strength, and for this reason we must plan the positioning of the radio equipment to avoid having to add lead weight ballast to the front or rear of the model to obtain the correct balance. The balance point of the model is critical to its flight characteristics and should be adhered to; it is allowable to come slightly forward of the indicated balance point, making the model less sensitive, but never, repeat never, let it balance further back than shown. A rearward balance point will result in a model that is over sensitive, liable to stall and drop a wing, in other words everything that the beginner does not want.

A suggested layout of radio equipment is shown on many plans. Unless the model is built very differently — and it should not be — the balance point should be quite near the optimum shown. The adjustment of the receiver and battery positions should be sufficient to obtain the required balance. We can use the plan therefore, for making up the pushrods and for positioning the servo bearers, on/off switch and cutouts for pushrod exits.

Radio equipment is not only expensive — (if you do not believe me ask **your** wife), but sophisticated and delicate electronic equipment that requires protection. It is in our interests to see that the equipment is efficiently instal-

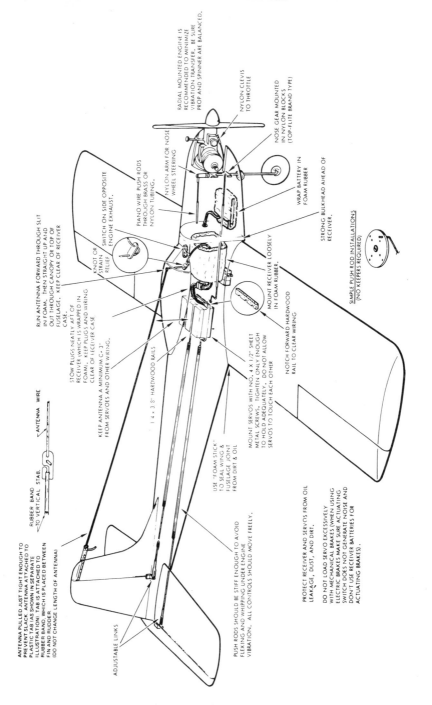

RADIAL MOUNTED ENGINE IS RECOMMENDED TO MINIMIZE VIBRATION TRANSFER. BE SURE PROP AND SPINNER ARE BALANCED.

NYLON CLEVIS TO THROTTLE

NOSE GEAR MOUNTED IN NYLON BLOCKS (TOP-FLITE BRAND TYPE)

NYLON ARM FOR NOSE WHEEL STEERING

WRAP BATTERY IN FOAM RUBBER

RUN ANTENNA FORWARD THROUGH SLIT IN FOAM, THEN STRAIGHT UP AND OUT THROUGH CANOPY OR TOP OF FUSELAGE. KEEP CLEAR OF RECEIVER CASE.

PIANO WIRE PUSH RODS THROUGH BRASS OR NYLON TUBING.

STRONG BULKHEAD AHEAD OF RECEIVER.

SWITCH ON SIDE OPPOSITE ENGINE EXHAUST.

STOW PLUGS NEATLY AFT OF RECEIVER (WHICH IS WRAPPED IN FOAM). KEEP PLUGS AND WIRING CLEAR OF RECEIVER CASE.

KNOT OR STRAIN RELIEF

MOUNT RECEIVER LOOSELY IN FOAM RUBBER.

SIMPLE PUSH ROD INSTALLATIONS (NO KEEPERS REQUIRED).

KEEP ANTENNA A MINIMUM C- 3" FROM SERVOS AND OTHER WIRING.

1 4 x 3 8" HARDWOOD RAILS

NOTCH FORWARD HARDWOOD RAIL TO CLEAR WIRING

MOUNT SERVOS WITH NO. 4 X 1/2" SHEET METAL SCREWS. TIGHTEN ONLY ENOUGH TO HOLD ADEQUATELY. DO NOT ALLOW SERVOS TO TOUCH EACH OTHER

USE "FOAM STICK" TO SEAL WING & FUSELAGE JOINT FROM DIRT & OIL

PROTECT RECEIVER AND SERVOS FROM OIL LEAKAGE, DUST, AND DIRT.

DO NOT LOAD SERVO EXCESSIVELY WITH MECHANICAL BRAKES (WHEN USING ELECTRIC BRAKES MAKE SURE ACTUATING SWITCH DOES NOT GENERATE NOISE AND DON'T USE RECEIVER BATTERIES FOR ACTUATING BRAKES).

PUSH RODS SHOULD BE STIFF ENOUGH TO AVOID FLEXING AND WHIPPING UNDER ENGINE VIBRATION. ALL CONTROLS SHOULD MOVE FREELY.

ADJUSTABLE LINKS

ANTENNA PULLED JUST TIGHT ENOUGH TO PREVENT SLACK. ANTENNA ATTACHED TO PLASTIC TAB (AS SHOWN IN SEPARATE ILLUSTRATION). TAB IS ATTACHED TO RUBBER BAND, WHICH IS PLACED BETWEEN FIN AND RUDDER (DO NOT CHANGE LENGTH OF ANTENNA)

RUBBER BAND TO VERTICAL STAB.

ANTENNA WIRE

led in the model and protected, as far as possible, from accidental damage. Most manufacturers supply with their radio outfits comprehensive instructions on the 'do's and don'ts' of installing their equipment. This information is based on practical experience and specialised knowledge and is written for your benefit. Read the instructions and adhere to them, if for no other reason than that by acting contrary to them the guarantee may be made null and void.

Battery pack

This is usually the heaviest item of the airborne radio equipment and is the most likely to create damage during a crash. Partially for this reason, and also for balance considerations, the battery pack is normally positioned in front of the receiver and servos. To help prevent damage, and reduce vibration effects from the engine, the battery pack must be surrounded by foam material. Foam plastic, unless of very high density, does not have sufficient resistance to crushing to be suitable for battery pack protection. As an experiment try holding a piece of plastic foam — the normal lightweight variety, between the thumb and forefinger and squeeze it. Very little effort is required before the thumb and forefinger meet, with no cushioning effect left. The inertia of a battery pack in even a minor crash is considerably greater than this pressure. Foam rubber, the lighter forms of rubber carpet underlay, are ideal for our purposes and the battery pack should be completely surrounded in this material secured lightly in position with adhesive tape or rubber bands. Do not bind the foam rubber too tightly to the battery pack or some of the vibration resistance will be lost. Take care not to strain the wires leading out from the pack, a sensible precaution here is to double back the wires and tape them to the pack.

Adhesive tape

Securing the lead from the battery pack.

I prefer models to have separate fuel tank and battery compartments but where the batteries are placed directly under the fuel tank the battery pack should, in addition to the foam rubber, be protected by wrapping in a polythene bag. This will prevent damage to the batteries should a leak occur in the fuel tank.

Receiver

The most delicate and most expensive part of the airborne equipment, the receiver, should be given special treatment. All too often, unfortunately, it is wedged tightly in a small area offering little or no protection from engine vibration or crash damage. The same principle of protection applies to the receiver as for the battery pack. Fortunately with less mass than the battery pack there is less inertia during a crash but, once again, foam plastic is barely

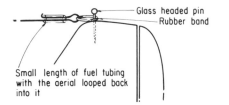

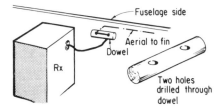

Retaining the end of the aerial at the fin.   Receiver aerial restraint.

good enough protection for the receiver unless it is very thick and dense. The foam wrapped receiver should be a 'loose fit' in the fuselage and should not be placed behind projections, such as switches, dowels, nuts and bolts; all possible causes of damaging a receiver in a crash. Position the receiver in the fuselage so that the servo and switch leads come in a convenient place, usually at the bottom of the fuselage, and for changing or switching the frequencies if these features are fitted.

Receiver aerials are necessary evils and although it would frequently be helpful, particularly in scale models, if we could cut them shorter or double them back on themselves this must never be done. To shorten an aerial at all will result in loss of range of the model and probably in the loss of the model too. Aerials should be routed directly out of the fuselage wherever possible and always kept clear of battery and servo wires. Taking the aerial to the tip of the fin is normally convenient and the aerial can be retained on the fin by using a small rubber band.

To prevent strain on the receiver aerial connection a 'stop' should be attached to the aerial wire where it exits through the fuselage. This can be made simply from a piece of 3/16 in. dia. dowel.

The aerial is looped through the dowel and 'slack' left between it and the receiver when the aerial is tensioned on the fin.

On/off switch
Never place the receiver switch where it will be affected by unburnt 'sludge' from the engine, always position it, if it is external, on the side away from the engine exhaust outlet. Most manufacturers supply the switch with an external plate with initials designating the on and off positions, if there is no plate make sure that you clearly mark on the side of the fuselage the respective on and off positions. I prefer to have the 'on' position to the rear of the fuselage so there is no risk of accidentally knocking the switch off during launching the model.

What better position to install the switch than internally in the fuselage. This gives us the problem of having to find some remote method of actuating the switch but this can be done quite simply as shown. Make the wire, projecting through the switch, long enough to ensure that it will not slip out when the switch is secured to the bulkhead with servo tape.

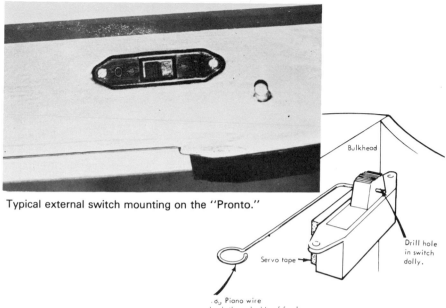

Typical external switch mounting on the "Pronto."

Bulkhead

Servo tape

Drill hole
in switch
dolly.

. . .d.. Piano wire
hook through side of fuselage

Installing the On/Off switch in the fuselage.

Servos

Before we can decide where to mount individual servos we must first check the operation of them and arrange them to give left rudder, when left rudder is applied on the transmitter, up elevator when the elevator stick is pulled back and fast engine when the throttle stick is moved upwards. Equally, to find this information we must work out the routes of the pushrods and linkages. It is common sense that the most direct route between the servo and control surface must be the best one and that to keep bends to a minimum is desirable. Unfortunately it is not usually as simple as that. The ideal arrangement for the linkages to the rudder and elevator is to have them crossing each other so that they exit directly to the control horns. This arrangement is not very often practical as, with the servos all at the same level, there is a risk of

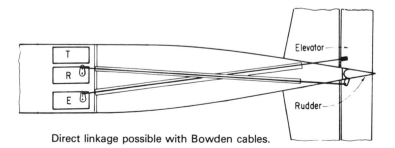

T

R

E

Elevator

Rudder

Direct linkage possible with Bowden cables.

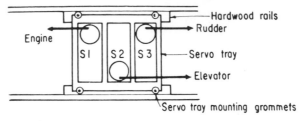

Servos mounted crosswise in fuselage.

pushrods fouling each other. By using cable in tube, or rod in tube linkages this method is both feasible and desirable as it prevents a sudden change of direction of the cable or rod after leaving the fuselage and connecing to the clevis. More frequently the pushrod has to exit the fuselage at an angle and to be straightened again to line up with the control horn. For training and sports models this is of no great importance as the air loads on the control surfaces are insufficient to flex or bend the wire pushrod ends. For faster models, pylon racers, aerobatic models etc., it is essential to keep these bends as shallow as possible. When working out the routes of the pushrods, and the side of the servo arm or disc to take off, remember that some radio outfits provide servos with opposite rotation thus giving a choice of servos for rudder and elevator operation to fit in with the most suitable layout. With rotary servos using arms, as opposed to discs, there may be a 'clashing' of arms if the servos are closely fitted in the same direction. This can easily be avoided by either reversing the fitting of one servo or changing the use of the servos. Once you have worked out the relative positions of the servos and the direction of operation mark each servo as to its purpose and direction, also mark the plugs on the receiver harness as to their function. The servos can be marked by writing on them with a chinograph pencil and the plugs by painting with enamel using a fine brush. Draw on the fuselage top view plan the rough positions of the servos, outputs and positions of take offs. It is now possible to draw directly onto the plan the position and lengths of the pushrods and we will consider the construction of them.

Pushrods

Should you prefer to use the nylon tube and cable or nylon rod then I would suggest following the manufacturers' instructions bearing in mind, once again, that the more bends there are the more 'slop' there will be and, para-doxically, the more friction too.

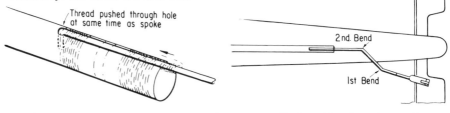

Binding to push rod dowel and clevis spoke.　　　　Push rod fitted to elevator horn.

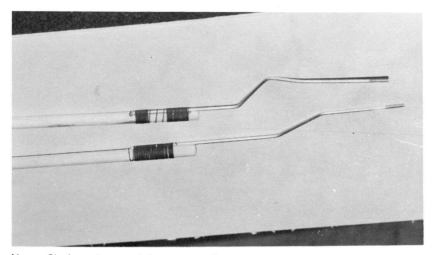

Above, Clevis spokes, ready bent, secured to push rods with glue and binding.
Right, Elevator horn should be in line with clevis rod.

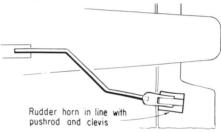

Rudder horn in line with
pushrod and clevis

Conventional pushrods were the earliest form of linkages between servo and control surface and, like the sewn hinges, still take a lot of beating. For the purpose of the **'Pronto'** ¼ in. dia. dowel and 15g. cycle spokes (or 16 s.w.g. piano wire) are just about ideal for the construction of the pushrods. The dowel can be from ramin wood (available from woodworkers shops) which is lighter and cheaper than birch dowel, it is also straighter grained with less risk of warping or having weaknesses of 'cross grain'. The dowel should take up as much of the total length of the pushrods as possible, bearing in mind that the dowel must not foul the rear former or end of the fuselage inside or hit the rear of the servos. Bending the cycle spoke at the rear of the pushrod is the first job, so start by screwing on a Micro Mold nylon clevis to the threaded end of the spoke until the end of the spoke just appears in the circular cut out in the clevis. Hold the clevis over the plan and mark the position of the first bend. Bend to the required angle by using heavy pliers, checking with the plan, and proceed to the second bend. Allow a further 1½ in. from the point where the dowel starts, for fixing the spoke to the dowel, and bend the final ¼ in. of the spoke at right angles and pointing down. The spoke for the rudder servo can also be bent, this is rather more

54" Basic trainer, the "Tyro Major", is suitable for two to four function radio and .19 to .29 size engines;

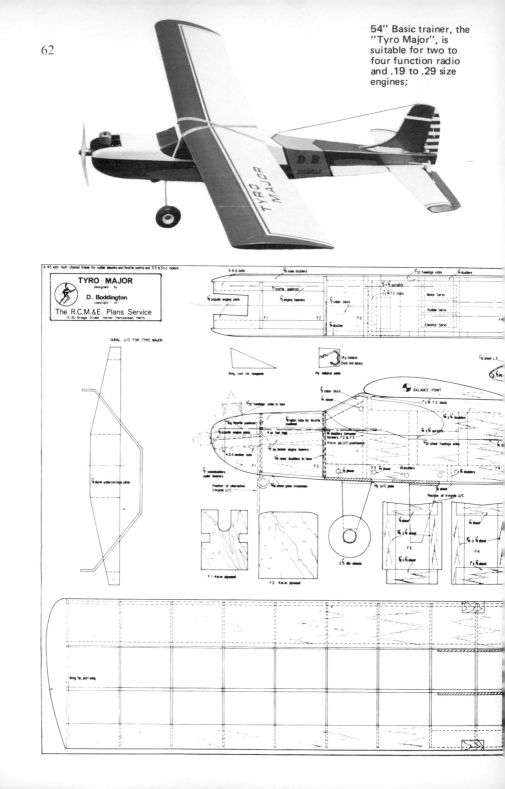

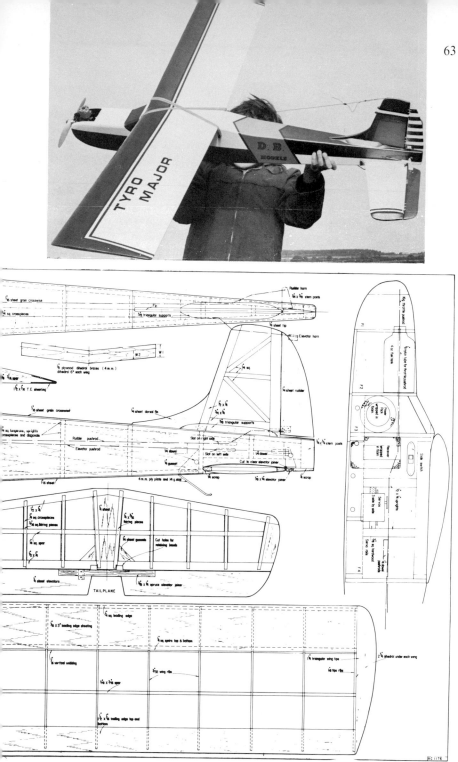

difficult as there are complete changes of direction and not on one plane only. It may mean you have to do a bit of 'jiggery pokery' to get this right but take satisfaction from the fact that it is probably the most difficult part of the construction you will have to face. When you are satisfied that the rear end spokes have been bent accurately remove the clevises. Cut the elevator and rudder dowels to the length you have drawn on the plan and, if the two are different lengths, mark them rudder and elevator to save confusion later. At a point 1¼ in. from each end of the dowels drill a 1/16th inch dia. hole, the holes at each end should follow the same line. Insert the bent over end of the spoke into the hole drilled in the dowel, at the same time inserting the end of 4-5 feet length of thread. Bind the thread tightly and closely around the dowel and spoke. To secure the opposite end of the thread, when the binding is complete, wind the thread round the spoke and pull it tight between the spoke and the dowel. Smear white P.V.A. glue or balsa cement over all the threaded area, rubbing it in well with your finger. The servo ends of the push-rods are treated in a similar way but with a straight piece of cycle spoke and not threaded. Leave the wire projecting about 1 in. beyond the servo arms or discs at this stage. When the glue to the four bound ends of the pushrods has dried remove the clevises. If the rudder and elevator control horns have not been fitted previously they should be fixed now. The positions are indicated on the plan but note that it is better practice to slightly angle the elevator horn to the line of the pushrod. Similarly, if not already cut, the slots for the pushrod exits should be made in each side of the rear fuselage. These slots should be about an inch long and 3/16 in. wide, remember to fuel proof the cut edges of the slot. Slip the pushrods down the inside of the fuselage and feed the threaded ends through the respective slots for the elevator and rudder, this is easily achieved with the tailplane and elevator off. Reconnect the clevises to the rudder and elevator horns on the second hole from the outside and check for full and free movement by operating the pushrods from the approximate position of the servos. The rudder needs to move about ½ in. each way measured at the bottom trailing edge, the elevator should move about ¼ in. either side of neutral. The masking tape we stuck around the elevator joiner and tailplane when making the hinges, is removed once the clevis has been fitted to the control horn. When all the movements are satisfactory, and minor adjustments made to the bends of the spokes as necessary, the pushrods can be removed again.

Heat shrink tubing (6.4 mm. dia. available from Radio Spares) can also be used on the pushrods to retain the wire ends. Firstly drill holes in the end of the pushrods—a Vee block holds the dowel satisfactorily when drilling with a pillar drill—and then file a small groove from the hole to the end of the dowel. Fit the wire into the hole and slip over a 1½ in. length of the heat shrink tube. Hold the tubing over an electric hot plate or a gas flame and the tube will shrink tight over the dowel and wire.

Throttle Linkages
The linkage between the throttle servo and the carburettor throttle arm is

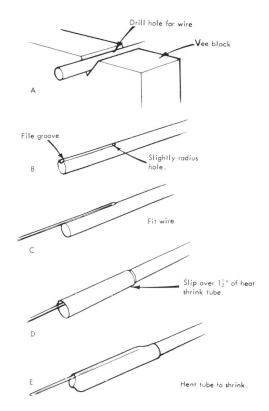

Rudder and Elevator horns and connections.

Right: Securing clevis rod to dowel push rod with heat shrink tube.

dealt with in a different way to the rudder and elevator, as there is normally insufficient space in the nose area of the model to fit in a conventional pushrod. We must also take care to eliminate, as far as possible, the ingress of oil and fuel residues from the engine.

The nose area around the fuel tank and engine, is often congested and needs careful planning of the route of the throttle linkages, this is made considerably more difficult when a steerable nosewheel is also fitted. As a general rule metal to metal linkages should be avoided on all control linkages. The reason for this is that, with the engine running, vibration can be set up causing the metal linkage to be constantly 'making and breaking' thus possibly producing spurious 'noise' signals that could interfere with the receiver. Some receivers are more sensitive to this type of interference than others but, for the sake of safety, it is better to avoid entirely a linkage involving metal to metal contact. I mention this here because it is sometimes difficult to fit a nylon clevis onto the carburettor throttle arm, on certain engines, and still obtain clearances for the throttle to operate. If you have to resort to using a piece of 16 or 18 s.w.g. wire, bent at right angles to go through the holes in the carburettor throttle arm, either the wire should first

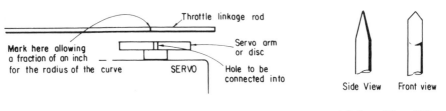

Marking the throttle linkage rod.   Forming drill from Piano Wire.

be sleeved with some thin plastic tubing (off a piece of electrical wiring) or a 'no noise' bush must be used.

To obtain accurate operation of the engine throttle we must arrange the total movement of the carburettor throttle barrel, to move through its full arc, and for this to coincide with the full movement of the servo, including transmitter trim movements. With the throttle lever on the transmitter fully up and with the trim lever also fully up the engine throttle barrel should be fully open i.e. looking down the carburettor air intake the hole in the throttle barrel should exactly coincide with the internal diameter of the intake. With the throttle lever on the transmitter fully back, but the trim lever still up, the throttle should be in a position to give the minimum safe idling revs from the engine. The movement of the trim lever to the down position should then be sufficient to cut the engine completely, giving us this safety facility should it be needed during flying. All of the foregoing may sound difficult to arrange but with the different hole positions on the carburettor throttle arm it is not too difficult to find the correct combination. We must be careful not to have the servo/linkage movement too great for the engine throttle otherwise there will be a strain on the servo at the extremes and cause overloading of the servos. The opposite may be the case with the linear output servos where there may be insufficient movement to operate the throttle fully. For this condition we must resort to incorporating a single arm crank in the linkage to increase the movement.

Wherever possible I would always recommend the use of a rotary servo for the throttle operation as it does give a much greater degree of flexibility.

The simplest form of throttle linkage is to use a rigid wire in a nylon tube assuming, of course, that the nylon tube will be following a straight line through the bulkheads between the radio compartment in the fuselage and the engine bay. If there are any curves and bends in this area, then a nylon tube and flexible braided cable must be used, but avoid any bends if at all possible. It is obviously better to plan the route of the nylon tube before commencing construction of the fuselage as the holes can then be drilled in the formers at this stage. To make the holes in the formers after the fuselage is complete will necessitate using a drill longer than is normally available so we must make our own. Cut a length of 10g. piano wire, for ⅛ in. dia. nylon tube, and simply file the end to a point.

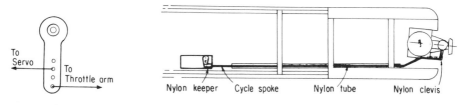

Simple crank to increase movement.   Installing the throttle linkage.

This makeshift drill will be quite efficient for drilling through balsa and plywood formers. The nylon tube should project about ⅛ in. in front of the engine bulkhead (F1), to avoid induced ingress of oil, and also project well into the radio compartment so that it passes the receiver position and does not allow the wire linkage to foul on the receiver packing. Nylon is not easily glued with epoxy resin adhesives and some adhesives that will hold nylon are, unfortunately, not fuel proof. A way of ensuring that the nylon is securely held at the former positions, and still remains fuel proof, is to first wrap the area of tube to be glued with a scrap of masking tape. The tape will adhere well to the nylon tube and the epoxy adhesive will bond the tape to the formers. Should you be unable to purchase suitable nylon tube there are some alternatives that can be used such as the internal ink tube from an old ballpoint pen. Do not however, use brass tube because of the metal to metal 'noise' problem.

For the wire connecting the servo output to the carburettor, a cycle spoke is again ideal as it already has the threaded end ready to receive the nylon clevis for the throttle arm. You may have a problem in finding a spoke of sufficient length, although they are available, alternatively, an extra piece of spoke or 16 s.w.g. wire must be bound and soldered to it, at the servo end. The layout of the throttle linkage should look like this:

The spoke should be bent at the throttle and then, with the clevis fitted, slipped through the nylon guide tube. Connect the carburettor throttle arm to the clevis and check for free movement from the servo end, there must be no binding of the spoke on any part of the engine. Leave about 1 in. of extra spoke length beyond the servo output hole for final connection and fitting.

Installing the Servos
Once again, when fitting the servos, we must bear in mind that ruination of electronic equipment—vibration. Servos should never be bolted or screwed 'hard' to any part of the fuselage as the vibration from the engine will travel through the fuselage structure straight to the servo. All servos are supplied with rubber grommets for mounting purposes and these should be used. A common fault of modellers in the screwing or bolting servos in position is to tighten up the screw or bolt too much onto the grommet thus compressing it and ruining its isolating effect. There should always by a little float between the washer, grommet and mounting rail.

In recent years the use of double-sided self adhesive servo mounting tape

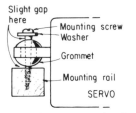

Mounting servo to hardwood rail.

Top Right. World Engines "Bantam Midget" servo features mounting lugs and grommet for installation, some servos have alternative types of mountings.

has become popular. The principle of mounting servos with this tape is that one side of the tape is stuck to the fuselage side or floor and the other side direct to the bottom or side of the servo. The method is simple but experts have very mixed views on the desirablity of using this form of mounting. Yet again, the reason for the doubts is vibration. Although the foam plastic tape absorbs some of the vibration shocks it still allows more vibration to be transmitted to the servo than can be considered ideal. One way to overcome this to some extent is to double insulate, i.e. the servos are mounted on a piece of plywood and the plywood is, in turn, mounted to the fuselage on double-sided foam tape. For the mounting, with tape, to be successful it is necessary to have complete cleanliness, there must be no trace of oil or dirt on the servo or on the wood. A nonporous surface is also required as mentioned previously. With servos mounted two or three abreast it is also wise to isolate them from each other by using a piece of wing seating tape (single-sided adhesive) stuck between pairs of servos. Mounting on tape naturally gives a flexible mounting and, without the cushioning effect of the wing seating tape, the servos tend to hit against one another. Servos can be stuck together as a 'block' by using the servo mounting tape between servos instead of wing seating tape. This makes a more "solid" mounting but also makes it extremely difficult to remove individual servos.

Servo Mounting Trays
Many manufacturers now produce, as an additional item in some cases, servo trays or mounting brackets to take one to three servos. Should trays or brackets be available for your type of servo I strongly recommend buying them, they make installing servos so much easier and more efficient too. There are a number of different patterns but the most common are for three servos abreast and two servos with one servo in front across the tray. Using a servo tray also gives us double vibration insulation as the servos are still mounted on grommets and the servo tray itself is fixed with grommets.

The servo tray is mounted on hardwood rails fixed across the width of the fuselage; alternatively the rails may be fixed on the side of the fuselage and the tray mounted with the servos facing across the fuselage.

Sprengbrook standard servo at left uses quick release individual mounting clip for installation in place of tray. Sprengbrook mini-servo with aileron installation tray seen at right.

Which type of servo tray to use and the method of mounting it, will depend on the most convenient layout for your particular servos, ⅜ in. beech or spruce is ideal for bearers either for servo trays or for mounting servos direct. The bearer must be securely attached to the fuselage side, this is very much

Servo trays for Sprengbrook micro servos. No mounting hardware is required — the servo mounting lugs key into the stops in the tray and are retained by the small vertical catches. The two larger trays each take three servos for the fuselage installations and two styles of fuselage installation tray are available. The one at left also mounts the on/off switch. Single servo tray bottom right is for wing mounted aileron servo.

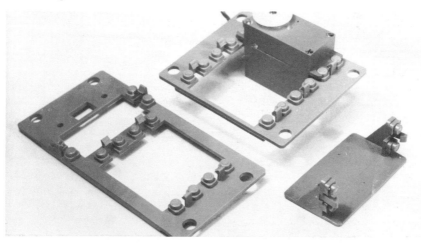

Servos may be mounted direct on to beech bearers fitted to the fuselage. Wood screws should not be overtightened to allow a resilient mounting to be maintained and less possibility of vibration being transferred to the servos.

easier when the bearers are glued lengthwise on the side of the fuselage. For bearers transversing the fuselage a small housing or support must be made for the bearer ends, end glueing to the side of the fuselage only is not good enough.

Accessories supplied with O.S. Cougar R/C system include neck strap, servo output discs, frequency pennant. Servo mounting clips at centre of picture come complete with mounting screws. In this case, the clips are at either end of spacers. Clips are screwed to transverse servo rails and spacers are cut away to achieve perfect clip spacing. Servos are located on vertical pegs and retained by quick-release clip at each end.

For mounting the servos directly on to bearers the spacing between the bearers must be accurate and it may be necessary to cut out small half-round notches to give clearance to the grommet and wires where they exit the servo cases. This is a tedious task, best performed with a rat-tail file, but is essential. Never force the wires past the bearers or there is a risk of pulling the wires from their internal connection or even fracturing them. Whether the rails are to support servos direct, or a servo tray, pilot holes should be drilled for all screw fixing. Use a drill one size smaller than the self-tapping screw so that the screw will enter the wood easily but still have sufficient purchase. Do not omit to drill these holes before fixing the rails in position, it is very difficult to drill them inside the fuselage and to attempt to force the screws in without predrilled holes will almost certainly result in the screw driver slipping and damaging the servo.

Epoxy is the best suited adhesive to glue the rails into position, the quick setting type will ensure you do not have to wait too long before carrying on with this interesting phase of the installation.

We have now reached the stage where the pushrods and throttle linkage is made, the hinges and control horns are fitted, the servo rails installed and holes cut for the switch and pushrod exits. We are now ready to install the equipment permanently—not quite! First we make sure we remove from the inside of the fuselage all traces of balsa chippings, dust, bits of wire, old screws and any other debris which, if left in there, will do a lot of no good to

Individual servo installation tray by West German Simprop R/C system manufacturer. Servo is located on vertical pegs and held in place with snap-on clip at either end.

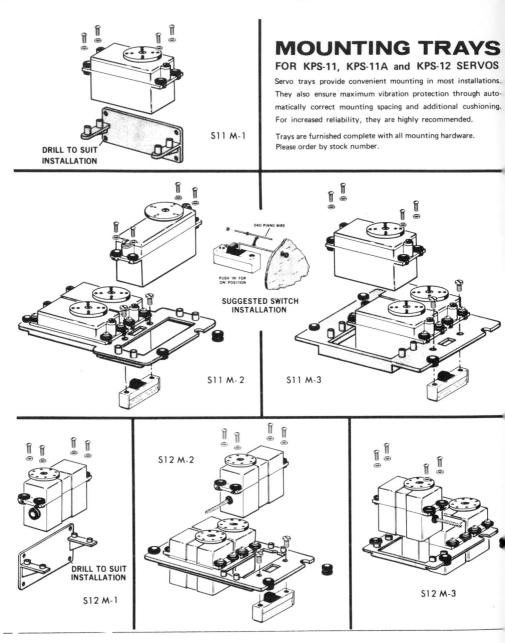

MOUNTING TRAYS

FOR KPS-11, KPS-11A and KPS-12 SERVOS

Servo trays provide convenient mounting in most installations. They also ensure maximum vibration protection through automatically correct mounting spacing and additional cushioning. For increased reliability, they are highly recommended.

Trays are furnished complete with all mounting hardware. Please order by stock number.

DRILL TO SUIT INSTALLATION

S11 M-1

040 PIANO WIRE

PUSH 'IN' FOR 'ON' POSITION

SUGGESTED SWITCH INSTALLATION

S11 M-2

S11 M-3

S12 M-2

DRILL TO SUIT INSTALLATION

S12 M-1

S12 M-3

KRAFT SYSTEMS, INC.

450 WEST CALIFORNIA AVENUE, VISTA, CALIFORNIA 92083
World's Largest Manufacturer of Proportional R/C Equipment

the equipment once installed. Bang the sides of the fuselage with the flat of your hand to remove the dust and, if you have it available, blow compressed air from a tube through the fuselage.

Commence the installation by first fitting the pushrods into the fuselage, through the slots and screwing on the clevises, remembering to leave room for adjustment in both directions. Do not attach the clevises to the horns at this moment but push the rods back as far as they will go and masking tape the servo ends clear of the servo positions. Screw the servos, or servo tray with servos installed, onto the bearers bringing the plugs and leads under the servos and towards the front of the fuselage. Take care not to trap any of the wires between the servo and bearer when screwing the servo down.

Connect the throttle servo first, slide the wire rod onto guide tube and attach the clevis to the carburettor throttle arm. Before cutting and bending the wire, to fit the other end into the servo arm, we must plug in the servos to the receiver and the receiver to the battery pack and switch on both the transmitter and the receiver. The receiver and battery pack can lie loosely in the fuselage for this purpose. Move the throttle lever and trim lever to the fully open position and manually open the carburettor throttle by pushing, or pulling as the case may be, on the wire linkage. We now have the servo and engine throttle in compatible positions. Just make one more check, by operating the transmitter throttle lever back and then forward again, we are about to connect the linkage to the correct side of the servo arm or disc. With

Plenty of room in the 'Pronto' for modern proportional equipment. Servos, receiver and battery positioned well forward to maintain the correct balance. Note that servo output arms may have to be trimmed on one side to avoid hitting the arm on the adjacent servo.

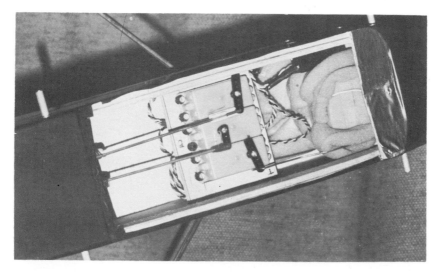

the wire held over the top of the hole in the servo arm (try the outside initially) mark with a soft lead or chinagraph pencil the position for the bend.

It may now be impossible to remove the rod to bend it, otherwise, after it's bent, it would be impossible to get it back through the guide tube. We must, therefore, carefully hold the wire and, with a heavy pair of pliers bend the end of the wire vertically upwards. The end of the wire is clipped off with wire cutters, to within ¼ in. of the bend. It may be necessary to remove the arm or disc in order to push the wire up from beneath the disc or arm through the hole. You may also find that the diameter of the hole, in the arm, or disc is too small to receive the wire rod, if so, drill out the holes carefully with the correct

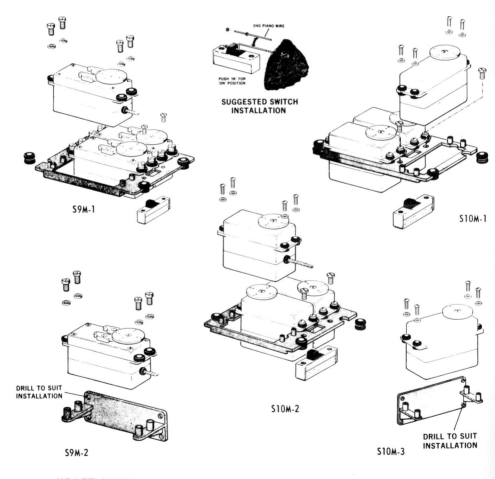

Simple installation in the "Tinker" biplane. Foam plastic padding on either side of fuel tank to prevent the fuel tank rotating.

size drill. Never attempt to drill these holes with the disc or arm connected to the servo, drills have a habit of suddenly 'grabbing' in nylon and you could easily penetrate the servo case by accident. With the servo disc or arm reconnected and the rod in position, retain the wire with a nylon keeper. Now check to see what carburettor throttle movement we are getting. If it is too small a movement, try fitting the clevis to a higher hole on the throttle arm. Should this still not do the trick you will have to obtain or make a longer servo arm, but this is very unlikely. For too large a movement, the linkage rod must be repositioned to a hole closer to the centre of the servo arm or disc. Do not forget that final bit of movement we require in slow throttle when we move the trim lever back to cut the engine. I am assuming that at this stage you have bench-run the engine and found the best slow speed settings; if not, you may have to make more adjustments to the throttle and linkage after the first flights.

On to the rudder and elevator pushrod connections. The clevises may now be connected to the respective horns and then a similar procedure is followed for marking, cutting and bending the wire as used for the engine throttle servo. The only two differences are that, this time, the sticks, trims and control surfaces want to be at neutral when marking the wire and that the pushrods can be removed from the fuselage for bending. The elevator and rudder pushrods should also be retained at the servos by nylon keepers. Small adjustments to centre the control surfaces by screwing the clevises in or out are acceptable but any appreciable miscalculation in pushrod length must be put right by binding on a new wire spoke at the servo end and remarking, bending and cutting. If you have followed the procedure carefully, this should not occur. Check that all the control surfaces are moving freely and in the correct directions, any serious binding will be noticed by the slowing down and 'labouring' of the servo motor. If this happens trace the fault (the pushrod exit may not be long enough for instance) and remedy the fault.

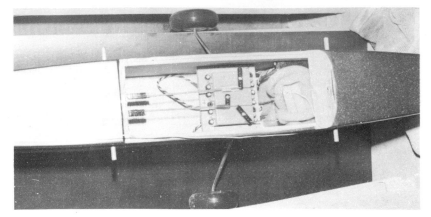

Servos mounted on a plywood board, specially moulded nylon servo trays are much easier to use and are more convenient.

Having reached the stage where everything is operating as it should we can permanently install the receiver battery pack and switch harness. With the foam rubber packing in place, position the battery pack and receiver as shown on the plan, the switch can be laid loosely on top of the receiver for the moment. Rubber band the wing in position, check the balance point, not by holding your fingers under the lower wing spars—this is too inaccurate a method until you are experienced at it. Get a piece of aluminium or thin dural about 4 in. long and ½ in. wide, bend it at the centre to the same dihedral as the centre of the wing. Drill a small hole in the centre of the bend and attach a piece of thread through the hole, knotting it on the underside. Slip the aluminium under the wing retaining rubber bands and slide it into position at approximately the balance point.

Suspend the model by the thread and adjust the position of the metal strip

Details of rudder and elevator connections to the "Pronto". Hinges formed from Kwik Cote.

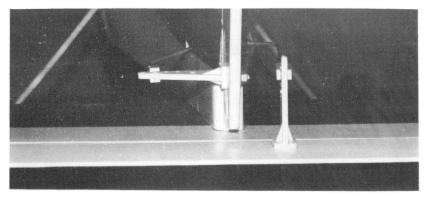

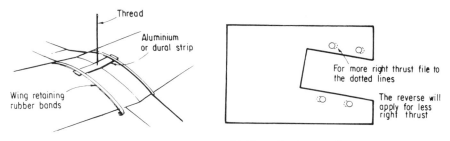

Finding the Balance Point.   Making side thrust adjustments.

until the model balances slightly in a nose down attitude—the centre of the metal strip is the balance point. Remember, slightly forward of the designed balance point—acceptable, further aft spells disaster. Slight adjustments to the battery pack and receiver positions are possible but any gross out of balance condition must be remedied by adding lead weights to the nose or tail. When lead weights are used, they should be fitted to underside of the engine mount or plate, and securely bolted to it, or to the front of the stern post and secured with epoxy and a woodscrew. With the correct balance point obtained the battery pack, receiver and switch harness can be permanenily positioned. The various leads from servos, receiver switch and the battery pack are neatly tucked away under the receiver foam, making sure that none of them is being strained. One lead that should be left easily accessible is the lead with the recharging plug on.

Engine Thrust Line Adjustment
Although it may be slightly out of context you will see, in the chapter on flight testing, that it may be necessary to make some adjustments to the engine down or side thrusts. For motors fixed on nylon or metal engine mounts it is a simple matter to place some large diameter washers between the mount and the front former or bulkhead. This can be satisfactory provided that only a small adjustment is required but over a degree or so of adjustment it would be better to use nylon thrust wedges. These are available in sets of 1°, 2° and 3° variations and should be positioned between the engine mount and the bulkhead for side thrust adjustment and between the motor lugs and the engine mount for downthrust, or upthrust, modifications. To make sidethrust adjustments for engines mounted on paxolin or Tufnol plates we can do one of two things. Elongate the engine mounting holes in the plate,—not the holes in the engine lugs, please!—or we can make a new paxolin engine plate. Downthrust variations are best dealt with by using the commercial nylon thrust wedges.

This chapter is, of necessity, a long one but it is essential to understand the importance of installing the equipment and linkages correctly. At first reading the advice and instructions may seem a little overwhelming but, if you take each item individually, there should be less confusion.

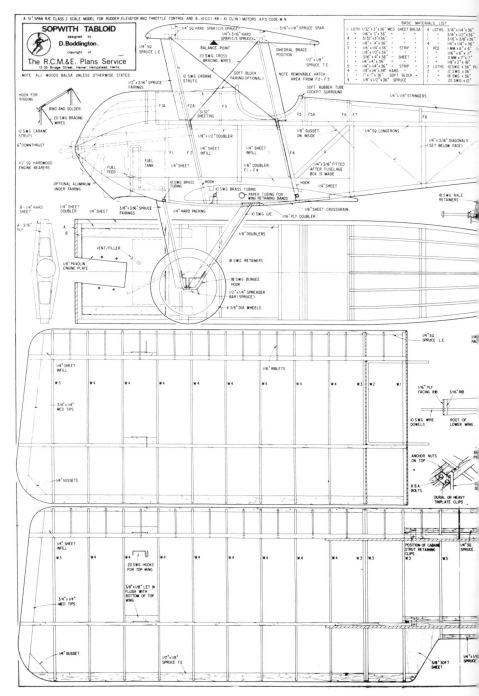

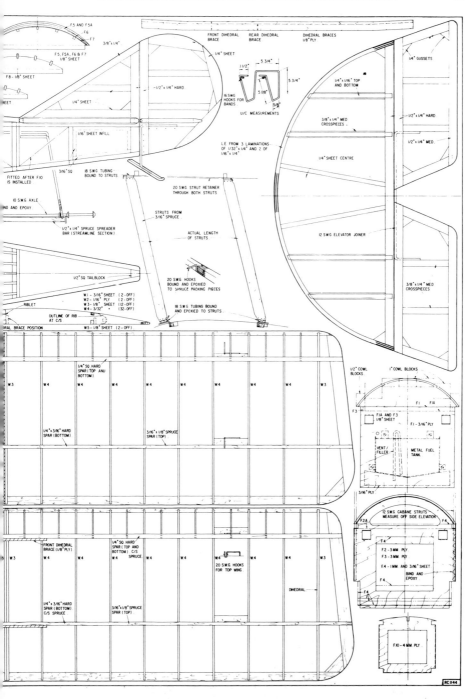

CHAPTER SIX

COVERINGS AND FINISHES

NATURALLY, WE all hope that our first model will turn out to be admired by our friends as well as being our own pride and joy. Nobody wants to finish up with a 'tatty' unattractive model but there is a vast difference between applying a lot of non-productive colour, purely for a 'surface' effect, and a neat, workmanlike finish. Particularly for the first model we should be concentrating on producing a durable and practical aircraft and decoration is a secondary consideration. Correctly applied covering, neatly carried out will, in any case, always look more attractive than a lot of badly applied paint.

The model may be covered in heavyweight tissue, Solar film or Kwik Cote or lightweight nylon although the latter is to be preferred for maximum strength. When tissue or nylon covering is used, the balsa framework should be brushed with sanding sealer and sanded between coats until a perfectly smooth finish is obtained. Coloured dopes or enamels should be kept to a minimum as this represents wasted weight, the model, however, should be thoroughly fuel proofed to avoid fuel seeping into the structure, particularly in the fuel bay.

Covering a model can be one of the trickiest parts of the construction although modern materials such as Solarfilm or Kwik Cote, and similar heat-activated plastic sheet covering materials, have made the process as simple as possible.

The secret of covering with tissue is to use as large a panel as can be attached without wrinkling, ending the panels where a definite break of contour appears (e.g. at dihedral breaks). Small pieces must be used for compound curves, (e.g. round fuselage noses, etc.). Only the outer edge all round needs to be pasted, except where concave surfaces occur, when the covering must be stuck to each individual member (e.g. each rib on the underside of an undercambered wing). The procedure is: 1) Cut a panel of tissue to the shape of the part, allowing 1 in. extra all round. 2) Apply paste (or cement) to the framework edges only except as above. 3) Lay the tissue lightly in place, press the centre of one end down and stretch along the length and press the centre of the other end down. 4) Stretch the tissue to the full width at the centre of the sides and press down, then work from this point to each end, adjusting the tissue so that all wrinkles are worked out. 5) Trim off to within ⅛ in. of the edge and paste the edge down. Completely cover a frame before shrinking, and always cover all woodwork, even sheeting. If water-shrinking is to be used, spray the water on with a Flit gun or similar, and allow to dry naturally over a period of 24 hours. Heavyweight tissue will require about three coats of slightly thinned dope to fill all the pores of the tissue before the colour dope or enamel trim colour and fuel proofer can be applied. It is more important to pin down the wings during the doping period to help prevent warping (twisting) of the wing panels. Because of pinning down, only one

Sopwith Tabloid, before covering. Scale model with traditional construction. This 1/6th scale model is suitable for .49 - .60 cu. ins. engines and is easy to fly. Plans on previous pages.

wing panel can be doped at a time but always the top and bottom of any panel or tailplane should be doped. Pinning down a wing panel is carried out by using small packing pieces at the pinning points, the wing need not be pinned down until the dope is just 'touch' dry, but it should then be left pinned to the board for at least six hours.

Lightweight nylon covering is applied in a similar manner to tissue but dope is more often used as the adhesive and the nylon is applied damp. Cut the nylon out, allowing an overlap of about ½ in. with the warp and weft running in line, or at 90°, with the wing span, fuselage datum, etc. Thoroughly wet the nylon and squeeze out the excess moisture in your hand and then spread the nylon out on some old newspapers. Apply plenty of dope to the framework to be covered and start applying the nylon at one end.

All parts that have been covered with nylon should be left for 24 hours before shrinking dope is applied. The first coat should be a heavy one with subsequent coats progressively getting thinner. Three or four coats will be needed until all the 'pinholes' in the nylon are filled in. When the nylon is being applied to the fully sheeted surface of the fuselage it should be started in the centre of the fuselage and worked outwards, with the aid of a wad of Kleenex tissues. I would suggest that for a first-ever attempt at covering, the tailplane, fin, rudder and elevators are covered first, followed by the fuselage and wing.

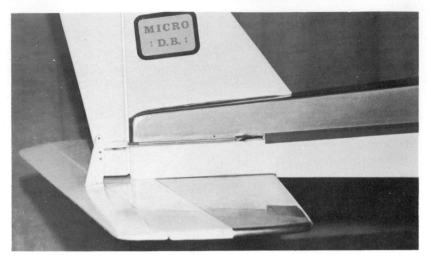

This 'Pronto' was covered in both Solarfilm and Kwik Cote, using these materials for hinges to the rudder and elevator.

Solarfilm and MicroCover

Experiments using plastic film materials had been made for some years by a number of individuals, with varying degrees of success, before the original Monokote came onto the market in America. This was the first really practical alternative covering to the conventional tissue, silk or nylon. The first British product to catch the market was Solarfilm and, since its introduction, has gradually improved and the range expanded, as also has Micro Cover. The 'instant' covering material is now a well established modelling product all over the world and although I shall refer to Micro Cover and Solarfilm in this chapter the comments will apply equally to similar commercial products of this type.

Solarfilm, Micro Cover and similar materials are high strength polymer plastic sheeting coated, on one side, with a coloured, heat sensitive adhesive. The adhesive side has a protective P.V.C. backing sheet to prevent accidental adhesion to other surfaces. Some of the advantages in using such a material, compared with conventional coverings, are:-

Ease — It requires less time in preparation of the model and in actual covering time.

Convenience — Because of the lack of strong smells and mess, covering can be carried out without incurring the wrath of the feminine members of the household.

Weight — The overall weight of the covering is low compared with silk or nylon covering. Having a smooth glossy finish the film is also very efficient from the drag point of view.

As with most materials there are some disadvantages, the main one being that it does not increase the strength of the airframe to any appreciable degree. It is important, therefore, to have a reasonably strong framework (although, in fairness, the same comment may be made when nylon covering is used, otherwise the structure may warp). The other disadvantages are of a minor nature such as the difficulty of covering in areas like the engine and fuel tank bays and small internal angles etc. With these problems it is chiefly a matter of gaining experience with the material and practising with a few spare pieces first.

Before covering is commenced any areas that are not to be covered, but will be exposed, i.e. the engine bay, should be doped, painted and fuel proofed to a matching, or contrasting colour. Polyurethane paint or enamels and fuel proofers are good for this purpose. The fuel proofing should extend a half inch or so inside the extent of the covering to give a safety margin. Always give the framework a careful wipe down with a dry cloth before applying the covering, as dust particles, trapped under the film, will mar the final appearance. The film is applied, after removing the protective backing, by ironing-on with a domestic iron and then warming to shrink the film tight and remove wrinkles. There are light, travelling type, irons available and these are particularly suitable, provided they are thermostatically controlled, for our purposes. These are easier on the wrist and arm muscles than some of the heavier domestic versions.

Two methods of covering can be used, the first being more suitable for open structures, i.e. unsheeted wings. Cut the sheet about an inch oversize

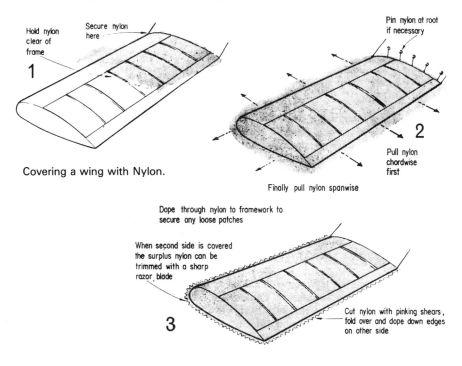

Hold nylon clear of frame

Secure nylon here

Pin nylon at root if necessary

1

2

Pull nylon chordwise first

Covering a wing with Nylon.

Finally pull nylon spanwise

Dope through nylon to framework to secure any loose patches

When second side is covered the surplus nylon can be trimmed with a sharp razor blade

3

Cut nylon with pinking shears, fold over and dope down edges on other side

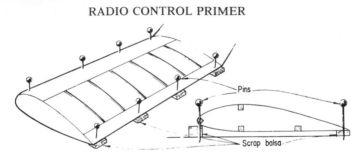

Pinning down the wing after doping.

and attach one edge to the structure i.e. leading edge of the wing followed by sealing the opposite edge, (trailing edge) pulling the sheet reasonably tight. The two ends, wing root and tip, are then sealed by applying the iron to the film at the edges. Temperature settings of the iron will be found by experience, it should be set at 'Rayon' or thereabouts and needs to be a slightly higher setting when shrinking, which is achieved by moving the iron to and fro across the surface without pressing down on the material. It is essential at all times of covering that the sole plate of the iron is smooth and free from nicks and blemishes. An alternative, and quicker, method of shrinking is to hold the covered panel in front of a radiant type electric or gas fire, but great care must be taken to ensure that the film is not overheated and melts. Despite this warning, I have no doubt that most modellers, using this method of shrinking, will burn at least one hole in some covering.It is sometimes necessary, when a structure it totally enclosed with an impervious heat shrink covering, to make a few 'pin holes' in the covering to allow the heat expanded air inside to escape.

Where fully sheeted surfaces are covered a different technique may be

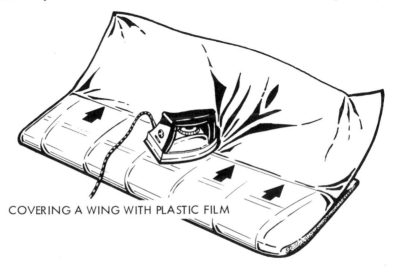

COVERING A WING WITH PLASTIC FILM

required and the covering is commenced from one edge and gradually applied, and tautened, across to the opposite edge. In this manner no air is trapped between the sheeted surface and the covering material and there is no risk of air bubbles forming. As the iron is pressing onto the sheeted covering to a great extent with this method it is advisable to protect the sole of the iron with paper tissues.

With sheeted surfaces gradually work with the iron from one edge to the opposite side.

Compound curves can be coped with using plastic films but a little experience and patience is required, a second pair of hands, to stretch the material over the curve, (i.e. wing tip or nose cowl) is also an advantage.

Always try to cover and overlap the film so that the joint is 'protected' from the airflow—and also fuel residues from the engine.

Heat Shrink fabrics

A development of heat shrink films is the introduction of heat shrink fabrics, such as Solartex and Coverite. They are applied in a similar manner to the film types but, being constructed from synthetic woven fabrics, have a much superior strength and puncture resistance. A slightly higher iron temperature is required for attaching and tightening the fabric and many modellers find the material easier to use than the film varieties. Costs are higher for the fabric materials, but are quite favourable compared with a nylon and dope finish, and the additional strength makes it very suitable for training models. Solartex is available in a range of colours (similar to self coloured nylons) and the finish is fuel proof. However, a coat of fuel proofer will help to protect the lapped joints and prevent oil and dirt becoming ingrained in the woven surface. The finish may also be doped and painted if desired.

Lapped joints, plain edges and all trim tapes, transfers etc. should be protected by a good coat of fuel proofer to help prevent the edges lifting.

To summarise, covering, for the uninitiated, may give more problems than most during the construction of the model. Whatever the method you use, try to take the covering stage steadily. You will probably reach a point where things will be going wrong and it may seem that you will never get the hang of it. Keep your 'cool', stick at it, work methodically and your efforts will be rewarded.

APPLICATION OF HEAT SENSITIVE
PLASTIC FILM COVERING TO A WING

Apply top surface with overlaps

TYPICAL 12% THICK CLARK Y AEROFOIL

Cover bottom of wing first

CHAPTER SEVEN

ENGINES, ACCESSORIES AND FIELD EQUIPMENT

FOR MANY YEARS the 'standard' engine for R/C model aircraft was the two-stroke glow plug engine, with the occasional diesel engine being used in small models. Two developments have changed this situation, the need for quieter engines and a movement towards larger scale and sports models. Environment requirements in many areas have enforced clubs and groups to take action to reduce the noise levels produced by model aircraft and although this can be achieved with two-stroke engines, by using larger propellers and efficient silencers, the four-stroke engine offers a pleasant alternative. Popularity of these engines is partially explained by the less offensive, and more scale like, noise they make and partially because of the engineering fascinations of the four-stroke. Being more complex they are also more expensive than the equivalent size two-stroke engine (a four-stroke

Engine mounting for the 'Pronto'. Enya 19 engine fitted.

An Enya 35 four-stroke engine,
one of several makes and
sizes now readily available and
increasingly used.

is less powerful per c.c., a '60' size engine gives approximately the same power output as a '40' two stroke) and they require more careful operating and maintenance. The two stroke glow engine is probably the easiest engine for the beginner to use initially; a four-stroke would be a good choice for a second engine.

Large capacity spark ignition and glow engines (15c.c. and above) have gained in popularity because of the desires of experienced R/C modellers to build large scale models. Converted chain saw engines started the movement towards bigger models and the model engine manufacturers now design specialist products for this end of the market. There is no denying that large models fly exceedingly well and impressively, they are also potentially more dangerous, by virtue of their weight and speed, and are not recommended for any but the most experienced of modellers.

Running-in a two stroke engine

The most important moments in an R/C engine's life are the first thirty or so minutes. Within this period the engine can be ruined or set fair for a long and reliable life. The main enemies at this period of running in an engine are lack of lubrication and overheating. Lack of lubrication is caused by using a fuel with too low an oil content, for running in, and overheating is a result of letting the engine run too lean (the needle valve closed too much) in the initial stages. Most commercial engines over the size of .40 cu. ins. are now ringed engines and do not require a great deal of running in, they must not however, be bolted straight into a model and run flat out from the word go. Smaller capacity engines, with lapped pistons, do require a little more in the way of bench running. It may be no more than a half-an-hour's running that is required but you soon begin to feel the engine loosening up. On flicking over a brand new engine you will notice that there is a certain 'stickiness' and the propeller does not go freely through one revolution. This tendency will reduce as the engine becomes more run in. Whether you are running in the engine in the model, or, preferably, for small engines, on the bench the advice is the same—Keep it running rich. About 25% oil content is what we must aim for in the fuel for running in purposes, the engine will throw a lot of oil out of the exhaust again but do not be tempted to reduce the percentage—it is needed to give the mating parts a chance to bed down without damage. It is certainly preferable to bench run engines before fitting them into the models as this gives a chance to get used to the handling characteristic, and find any faults, before permanently installing them. It is also preferable to run the engine without the silencer during running in, remember that the engine must be kept as cool as possible at this time and a silencer has the effect of retaining the heat of the engine. You may not be too popular with the neighbours when running an engine for prolonged periods in the garden shed—particularly unsilenced—but an aid here is to fill a biscuit tin, or similar receptacle, with old rags and foam polystyrene and position it at the side of the exhaust outlet. This will absorb quite a lot of the sound.

Positioning the fuel tank for a bench is as important as it is in the model so make sure it is mounted on the same level as the engine carburettor and not too far away. Whatever the manufacturers may say, open up the needle valve a minimum of four or five turns. Prime the engine, by placing the finger over the air intake and sucking in fuel by turning over the propeller three or four times. The propeller, for right handed people, should be set at 'twenty minutes to two' when viewed from the front. It is virtually impossible to describe, in words, how to flick a propeller over to start an engine; mostly it is a matter of practice and feel. Most modellers use their index finger (the finger next to the thumb) for 'flicking' the propeller over the compression stroke although some prefer a two finger flick. To a considerable degree the faster the propeller is turned over the more likely it is to start and the new range of electric starters certainly make life easier in getting reluctant engines to burst into life. With the plug connected to the booster battery, which must be well charged, start to flick the propeller over in an anti-clockwise direction—viewed from the front. The chances are that it will take quite a bit of flicking initially before it burbles into life—and burble is just what we want it to do. Once it is running try removing the plug clip, if the engine splutters to a halt turn the needle valve down a quarter of a turn and try again. Once it is running at a stuttering four stroke leave it to run the tank full through; keeping an eye on it in case it shows any signs of speeding up towards a two stroke. On the following runs you can start to turn the needle valve down for a few seconds at a time, so that it is just breaking between four and a two stroke. For a .19 cu. ins. engine about a half-dozen 4 oz. fuel tanks should be sufficient to free the engine, you can bring it into a two stroke for short periods during the last two or three tanks full. Never let the engine stop by getting to the end of the tank, and thus gradually leaning out the fuel mix to the engine. To stop the engine put your finger over the air intake and choke it to death instead, but take care not to put your finger in the propeller accidentally. Another advantage of running your engine on the bench is that you will be able to find the optimum settings of the throttle ready for fixing

The "business end" of the "Sky Rider" prototype fitted with an O.S. 40 engine and Horizon four function radio.

the engine servo linkage when it is installed in the model.

With the engine installed in the model continue to treat it with a lot of respect during flying for the first hour or so. Have it 'singing' between a two and four stroke for most of the time only gradually easing it into a full blooded two stroke. Keep an ear open for that tell-tale slight hunting variation in the engine note when it is two stroking—a sure sign that the needle valve is set too lean. A continued lean run is no good to an engine at any stage of its life and if you see signs of discoloration on the cylinder head you know that you have been 'over cooking' it. When you think that the engine may be too lean during flight throttle back immediately, land and adjust the needle valve—do not be tempted to continue flying with the engine lean although throttling back slightly may be sufficient to cure the problem.

Many times I have heard a modeller bemoan the fact that his engine started perfectly when he tried it at home yet, at the field, starting presented problems. Frequently the problems of starting are accentuated by cold weather and, an engine that gives few problems in summer conditions can become distinctly temperamental when the temperature drops. Assuming that the basics are correct i.e. the plug is sound, the starting battery is well charged and the leads and contacts are clean, there are one or two 'tricks' that we can use to assist starting stubborn engines. A small prime of diesel fuel will often, because of the ether content, encourage an unwilling engine to burst into life. Commercially available 'Quick Start', used for cars, will have the same effect. Use of a mild nitrated glo fuel (3-5% Nitro Methane), certainly assists the engine to fire and run smoothly and it is always worthwhile experimenting with different types of plugs and propellers to find the one that gives the best starting, running and idling.

Propellers
Propellers are designated by diameter (distance from tip to tip) and pitch (the distance the propeller would move forward in a 'solid' body for one revolution). The engine manufacturer's instructions will suggest suitable propeller sizes but the optimum will depend on the type of model and can only be found out by experience. Propellers are normally manufactured from three different types of materials—wood, Nylon and glass fibre.

You will see all serious competition modellers using wooden propellers. They are the most efficient, are rigid and can be prepared to a high finish. They have one big disadvantage—they break easily if the model tips over on landing or in a crash, this can make learning to fly rather expensive. Nylon propellers are much more resilient and are unlikely to break on landing unless there is a severe nose in, with the engine running. Nylon propellers too have disadvantages. Being flexible, the pitch (angle of the blade) tends to vary in flight and the efficiency is, therefore, lower than that of a wooden propeller. This is not a serious deficiency for sports flying. The main disadvantage, and danger, is that in the manufacturing moulding process it is possible to build up internal stresses in the nylon. The only way these stresses can be eliminated, and then not always totally, is by ageing. When you buy a propeller it is impossible to tell how much natural ageing has taken place so it is safer to artificially age it. This can be achieved by boiling the propeller in water for a period of ten to fifteen minutes which should remove most of the internal stresses. Always treat nylon propellers with a great deal of respect, they could shatter at any minute—more so in cold weather, and never stand in line with the spinning propeller disc when the model is on the ground. To me, it is frightening to see a modeller leaning over the top of a nylon-propellered engine to make an adjustment to the carburettor. Should the propeller disintegrate there is considerable risk that a piece of the propeller could hit him in the face.

Fuel Tanks
Nearly all fuel tanks used in R/C models are of the 'clunk' type, so called because of its weighted fuel pick up on a flexible tube. The basic design of the clunk tank has varied little since its inception many years ago, the changes being limited to minor improvements and the shape of the polythene tanks. The operation of the clunk tank is self evident but there are a few things to watch for. It is difficult to find a suitable material for the flexible feed line, when high nitro fuels are used, which will not 'grow' and has just the right amount of flexibility to bend back on itself without 'kinking' and starving the engine of fuel. Keep an eye on all flexible fuel tubing, a small pinhole anywhere in the feed line can cause very erratic running of the engine.

Positioning the tank in relation to the needle valve on the engine is most important. Firstly, the tank should be located as close to the engine as practical, the fuel feed line to the carburettor should also be as short as possible but without any sharp bends. The most important factor is the

Two "Tinker" biplanes, one fitted with a 1.5 cc diesel engine for two function radio. The model in the background used three function radio and a .15 cu. ins. glow engine. A very stable and easy model to fly.

height relationship between the centre line of the tank and the needle valve. Engines vary enormously in the variation of fuel head they will accept, some are not sensitive about it, others are very critical. High performance engines, with large air intakes and poor suction, are the most critical. With a tank centre line mounted above the valve you will have an engine that may be difficult to start because it is flooding, it will also tend to run rich for the first part of the flight. For starting, with a high fuel tank position, keep the tail of the model well down to prevent flooding.

Most engines will accept a small fuel suction, i.e. the centre line of the fuel tank below the needle valve by up to a half inch. An assistance in overcoming the differential tank leads is to use a pressurised fuel system. Nearly all engines or silencers are now fitted, or supplied, with a nipple to allow tubing to be taken from it to the vent on the fuel tank. After filling the tank, the pressure line is connected and the filler must be sealed off—a screw inserted in the flexible tube on the filler pipe is fine. Once the engine starts the pressure created in the silencer keeps the fuel at a slight positive pressure throughout the flight and often results in a more consistent engine run.

One other source of engine malfunctioning, and an inconsistent engine can be most frustrating, is dirty fuel getting to the needle valve and clogging the small orifice. The way to avoid dirty needle valves is to clean the fuel when pouring it into the main container, fitting a filter in the container and a further filter, either in the form of the clunk weight in the fuel tank or between the tank and the carburettor, in the feed line to the engine.

Field Equipment
With all the excitement of learning to fly your model it is easy to overlook the preparation of the tools and spares that may be needed at the flying field. It is

most annoying to arrive at the flying field and find that you have forgotten one vital piece of equipment. Ideally. one should have an inventory written out, pinned on the side of the field box and protected by a covering of clear polythene. A quick check of the contents, before you set off, will ensure that nothing will be missing, unless there is a major disaster on the flying field.

A well established and stocked field box is of primary importance although I have to admit that I am one of the worst offenders as regards arriving at the flying field with a minimum of accessories—usually what I can store in my pockets.

Here are some of the items of equipment and tools that you will require:—

(1) The complete model, transmitter, aerial and frequency flag.

(2) Pliers, wire cutters, screwdrivers, plug spanner, small adjustable spanner, small box spanners, small file, knife, razor blades, balsa cement, quick set epoxy glue, nuts, bolts and washers, clips, pins, thread and pencil. Detergent squeeze bottle (for cleaning down the model) cleaning rag and paper towels.

(3) Clean fuel, fuel filling bottle, fuel 'squirt' primer bottle, fully charged battery, glow clip and cable with plug testing facililty, spare glow plugs, fuel tubing, alternative and spare propellers, starter or finger stall guard.

(4) Rubber bands, Plasticine and lead for balancing adjustment.

(5) For single channel model only—winder for escapement rubber, spare escapement rubber, .8 mm 1 mm and 1.5 mm plywood for wing and tail-plane packing. Thin aluminium sheet for trim tabs. Tuning tool for receiver tuning, spare batteries for the receiver.

(6) If your club or group do not supply it, a small first aid tin should be carried. It only needs to contain basic items sufficient to deal with cuts and abrasions, etc.

(7) You may also wish to allow room for carrying liquid refreshments—of any type you fancy.

Field boxes seem to come in two types, one being fairly small and compact and without the facility for resting the model on top for starting purposes. The other type is a fairly large affair, not quite so elaborate and 'compartmentalised' but capable of being sat upon—not a consideration to be ignored—and for the model to be rested upon. An alternative to the purpose made field box are certain containers, designed for other purposes, that can be readily adapted to our use. The metal tool box, with the hinged lids and collapsible tool trays, is an example. Another container that is most suitable for a field box is the 'baby box' designed to carry all the impedimenta required for nursing a young baby. These plastic boxes, with metal carrying handles, have trays and require little adaption to our needs.

CHAPTER EIGHT

PREPARATION AND FLYING

The Moment—Nearly

ONE OF THE biggest problems with flying, as we shall certainly find out, is disorientation. Disorientation simply explained, is being unsure of which way the model is going and, when we do know which way it is going, which control to apply i.e. is it left rudder or right that is required? There is no substitute for experience to overcome these problems but to gain this experience on the flying field can be very expensive. Our homework consists of suspending the model from the ceiling, switching the receiver and transmitter on, viewing the model from all angles and finding the correct signals to give to make the model take certain actions. Now if the wife, children, neighbours or girl friend see you doing this they will almost certainly think that you are stark raving mad, so pick a time when you are on your own—you will need all your concentration anyway.

You can use the same metal bar that we used for balancing the model previously, for suspending the model but do ensure that the cord is firmly attached to the ceiling or light. A second line can be taped to one wing tip and tied to a convenient point to steady the model to one angle. Alternatively, if you have a cooling fan handy, it may be possible to produce enough airflow over the control surfaces to allow them to function to some degree (a la wind tunnel). With this system the second line should not be fitted as the single suspension point will allow the model a certain degree of 'freedom.'

With everything switched on, view the model from behind and watch the controls move as you move the control levers. Consciously think of giving left or up or slow motor etc., don't just sit there waggling the sticks. Do the same from the front of the model, noting that the model turning to the left is turning to your right. Get used to realising this factor so you won't be caught out when you are actually flying the model. Keep viewing the model from all directions, so you are sure you will recognise which way it is flying when you are out at the flying field on your own. Get used to operating all the controls on the transmitter, including the trims, without having to look for them; in fact so that it is automatic. In other words, keep at it until you feel really comfortable with the transmitter in your hands and you know at a glance which way the model is flying.

AND SO, the day of reckoning! . . . or more likely to the days of frustration when the model is complete and you are ready to go, but the weather is no good, or the wife wants you to take her out. One thing is certain, it will pay to wait for the right day when there is only a light wind blowing and your mind

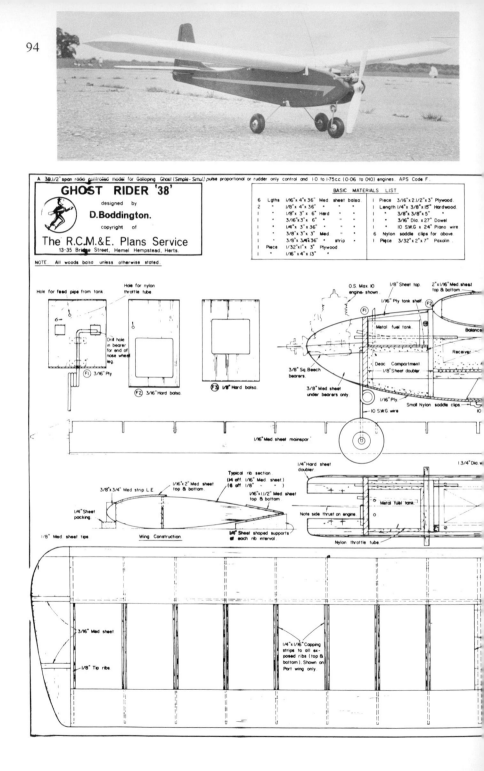

A 39.1/2" span radio controlled model for Galloping Ghost (Simple-Simul) pulse proportional or rudder only control and 1·0 to 1·75 c.c. (0·06 to 0·10) engines. APS Code F.

GHOST RIDER '38'

designed by

D. Boddington.

copyright of

The R.C.M.&E. Plans Service

13-35 Bridge Street, Hemel Hempstead, Herts.

NOTE   All woods balsa unless otherwise stated.

BASIC MATERIALS LIST

6 Lgths	1/16"x 4"x 36" Med. sheet balsa.	
2 "	1/8"x 4"x 36" " "	
1 "	1/8"x 3" x 6" Hard	
1 "	3/16"x 3"x 6"	
1 "	1/4"x 3" x 36" "	
1 "	3/8"x 3"x 3" Med "	
1 "	3/8"x 3/4"x36" " strip	
1 Piece	1/32"x1"x 3" Plywood	
1 "	1/16"x 4"x 13" "	

1 Piece	3/16"x 2.1/2"x3" Plywood.
1 Length	1/4"x 3/8"x15" Hardwood.
"	3/8"x 3/8"x 5" "
1 "	3/16" Dia. x 27" Dowel
1 "	10 S.W.G. x 24" Piano wire
6	Nylon saddle clips for above
1 Piece	3/32"x 2"x 7" Paxolin.

Ghost Rider 38. Designed originally for single channel, pulse proportional, it is equally suitable for proportional equipment. Very aerobatic with a .10 or .15 cu. ins. engine. One of a series of designs by the author, including the "Ghost Rider 50" and "Sky Rider".

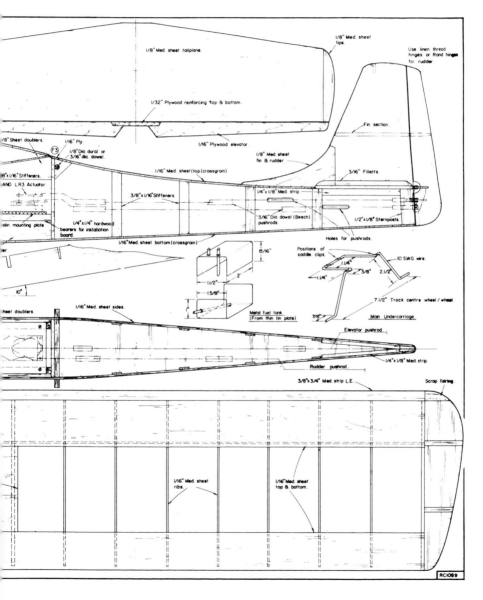

is not concerned with other matters. So, as we probably have a few hours to spare before that first flight let us take another look at the basic aerodynamics discussed in Chapter 2, the flying instructions, and make a final check of the model and the operation of the radio control equipment.

Having ensured as far as posssible, that everything is working as it should, we will now consider the instructions for the flying field. Because the most difficult group of would-be R/C flyers are the ones who have no previous aeromodelling experience and have no experienced modeller to help them, the instructions will be directed mainly to them.

At the flying field

Your first duty on reaching the flying field is to generally survey the surroundings and consider the weather conditions. Note the wind direction and strength, then position yourselves in the field clear of obstructions; bearing in mind that launches and take-offs should always be into the wind. The larger the flying field the better, but if you are limited in the size of the field available, aim to fly from a spot about two-thirds upwind and slightly to the left of centre when facing into wind.

The reason for this position is that the glide on the landing approach can take more distance than the climb away from a launch, and it is generally easier to land the model with the pilot on the left of the model, with both facing into wind. Make sure that the weather coming up does not look too fierce and that you are not likely to be caught by a sudden squall. Never fly just before dusk because darkness can fall very rapidly and it is easy to lose sight of the model or at least the sense of direction . . . . orientation we call it. Hoping for really good weather, we did remember to bring our sunglasses didn't we? A model under only partial control and passing in front of the sun can be a very embarrassing situation without them.

Having set up our equipment, we must now carry out a range check on the radio equipment, in accordance with the manufacturer's instructions. Make sure first that you and your helper understand and agree any hand signals to be used to indicate the operation of the controls. With this completed we can now finish rigging the model and prepare the engine for starting.

Remembering that we shall be flying the model in a left-hand circuit and landing on our right-hand side (when facing the wind); check the flying area to make sure that it is clear of obstructions and spectators. The latter items are best dispensed with entirely on the first few flying occasions, they invariably say the wrong thing at the right time.

Most dangerous periods of all forms of flying are the times at launch and landing so try to 'keep your cool' at these moments. If at any time you feel yourself getting flustered (except when actually flying), give it a rest—have a walk round and just calm yourself down.

The **'Pronto'** can be test glided to check that the flying trim is reasonably correct, but I do not advocate this for the inexperienced modeller and helper. It is unlikely that the standard of launch and test glide would be good enough for the unpractised eye to obtain any useful information from it. It is more important that the model should be built accurately and balanced correctly as it is unlikely then to be grossly out of trim. A limited amount of fuel only should be put into the fuel tank, sufficient for about five minutes total time, i.e., two minutes running on the ground and three minutes flying time.

With the engine started, adjust the needle valve so that it is running rich at something like two thirds of full revs. This will be achieved by opening the needle valve from ¼ to ½ a turn beyond the setting that gives the engine maximum speed. Check this setting by holding the model in a vertical, nose-up attitude. The engine should still run slightly rich without speeding up to a full two stroke run. If it does speed up in this attitude, open up the needle valve further until the motor continues to just four stroke while in the vertical position. When the engine is running satisfactorily, switch on the transmitter and receiver, being careful to ensure the switch on the model is pushed fully home. Your helper now picks up the model and faces into wind while you take up a position about five yards to the rear and slightly to the right of the model. In this position you will be able to see what is going on while positioned out of the direct blast from the propeller. Check carefully that all the controls are working correctly: left rudder, right rudder, up elevator, down elevator and, if it is fitted, throttle control. Flying instructions given here are based on a 'Pronto' without ailerons fitted, with ailerons these can be used in lieu of the rudder. Incidentally, if you have engine control it is better, for the first flights, to arrange the throttle to stop the engine com-

Shoulder and high wing models are easier to hand launch than low wing designs.

pletely when slow throttle position is selected at the transmitter without
having to resort to the trim as well. Now, with all systems go, it is time for
your helper, at a prearranged and positive signal from you, to launch the
model. Do make sure that the signal to launch, and one **not** to launch, is fully
understood — many a model has been launched when the pilot was really
trying to indicate to the helper that he wanted the engine stopped.

Your assistant must hold the model in his right hand (assuming that he is
right handed — and that applies to all of the other instructions) by the
bottom of the fuselage, underneath the balance point. If there is a wind
blowing, he may steady the left wing tip with his left hand but this steadying
grip should be taken away before the actual launch action. At your signal to
launch, he must then run forwards as smoothly as possible and launch, or
push, the model into the air. The launch must be level in all respects with the
wings level and the nose of the aircraft pointing neither at the ground nor
into the sky. The model must also be launched at a reasonable speed otherwise a stall will occur and all control will be lost. It is difficult to indicate in
words the speed of a launch but, when running forward at a steady rate the
model will still require an additional push to get it safely airborne, only in
stronger winds will it tend to fly out of your hand. One of the biggest faults is
to throw the model upwards, for some reason a lot of launchers seem to
assume that if you throw it upwards it has a better chance of staying up there.
In fact, this brings the model very near to the stalling point and with the
result that the pilot has to be quick to ease in some down elevator to level the
model out.

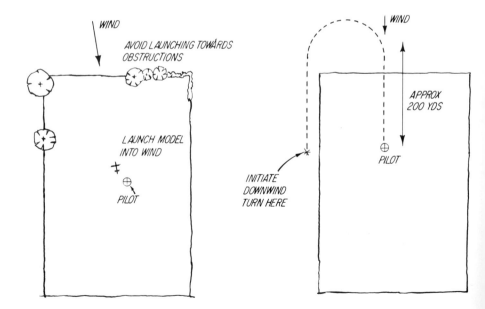

Check the operation of all controls, with the engine running, before launch.

Perhaps, by now, you are already terrified at the thought of launching a model! Try not to be. To some it will come easily and to others of us, including myself, it will never be 100 per cent.

From the instant at which the model leaves the launcher's grip we are in the hands of the builder, designer and, most of all, the pilot. From a good

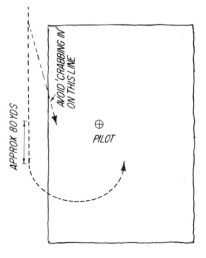

Left to right, sketches show procedure for a left hand circuit from launch to landing. In windy conditions the downwind turn must be initiated at an earlier stage.

launch the model will probably dip a little (i.e. sink toward the ground for a foot or so) and then, as the speed builds up, start to climb away. With luck it will climb steadily and fairly straight. Should this occur, do not attempt to control the model at this stage. There is always the temptation to 'tweak' a lever just to make sure that everything is working but it is safer if we can avoid making corrections when the model is still close to the ground and flying fairly close to the stalling speed.

What if it does not climb away nice and straight? Let us consider the alternatives.

(a) The model dives fast for the ground. — This is unlikely unless the model is considerably out of trim with too much down elevator. But, should it happen, you will need to be very quick to feed in some up elevator. The chances are that in your hurry to take corrective action you will pull in full up elevator in which case you must then be ready to level out the model again when it is climbing away steeply, otherwise a vicious stall will result.

(b) A turn to the left or the right. — The turn or bank may be a result of a poor launch or due to incorrect trimming of the model. Whatever the cause, correction of the turn, if at all severe, must be made, but try not to give full control deflection, rather just sufficient rudder to straighten the model again. If the turn is a result of the model being out of trim, then obviously a small amount of corrective rudder must be retained from this point on.

(c) Climbing too steeply. — What is too steeply? It is difficult to define in terms of degrees to the horizontal as the other factors of thrust of the engine and weight of the model have to be considered. If the model is trying to climb at an angle of $45°$ or more then you can certainly expect trouble. The other indication of an excessively steep climb is that the model will slow down rapidly, and, unless corrected, will stall with insufficient height to recover speed and control before the model hits the ground.

Obviously we must correct this excessive climb by applying down elevator, but how much down elevator will depend on the position and speed of the model at the time of application. If the down elevator is only fed in as the model reaches the stall, it will not be very effective and full control will be needed, because the faster the model is travelling, the more effective will be any control applied. Of course, if you have both elevator and rudder correction to make after the launch, you have really got your hands full — I hope your homework will have been some use to you.

Having recovered from the initial shock of being responsible for controlling the model in front of you, it is now your aim to gently climb the model directly up-wind until we are at a reasonable height (say three or four houses high) and about two hundred yards upwind. At this point we can start to initiate a $180°$ turn to the left by moving the rudder left on the transmitter about half its total movement. The aim must be to execute a gentle turn with the model never banked over more than $30°$. We shall probably find that the model takes a little time to react after the initial movement of the rudder lever and then the turn of the model gradually increases with the angle of

The launch must be level in all respects and firm enough for the model to gain flying speed.

bank also increasing. We must, therefore, be ready to reduce the amount of rudder applied.

Should we, due to inexperience, let the turn increase until we have a very steeply banked turn, we will probably notice another thing happen to the model—the nose will drop. We now have a model in a spiral dive and the automatic reaction is to pull back on the elevator lever to make the model climb again. This is a most dangerous thing to do, as described in the explanation of basic aerodynamics, and the model must be straightened from the turn before the elevator is used to get the model out from the dive.

With the model now heading down-wind we must prepare to carry out our second 180° turn to bring the model overhead and facing upwind again. This turn is initiated when the model is level with the pilot.

Again the model may take a while to start the turn, the more so apparently, if there is a wind blowing. Continue flying in these left hand circuits and gaining height until the fuel runs out. During the upwind runs there should be an opportunity to correct any trim problems by using the rudder and elevator trims at the transmitter. Rather than taking your hands off the rudder and elevator levers, to move the trim controls, it is probably safer to get your helper to move them for you.

Explain beforehand to your assistant where the transmitter trims are and which way they move.

When the engine finally cuts, give the model a few seconds to settle into its natural descending attitude before moving the controls. The aim now must be to continue the left hand circuit and glide down to an upwind landing. Whether we do one or more circuits on the glide will depend on the height of the model when the engine cuts, but our intention must be to position the model travelling downwind and level with us, at a height of about three houses. From here we allow the model to travel a further 60-80 yds. downwind (less in windy conditions) before commencing the final turn into wind. Beware, on the downward leg, of 'crabbing in' towards the field as this will necessitate an excessively steep final turn. Complete the final turn by heading directly into wind, i.e. aiming slightly to the left of you as you look at the model.

Providing the model is lined up into wind as it levels off from the final turn, we can concentrate on the elevator control and only need to make minor corrections to the rudder. Do not worry if your model appears likely to land some distance away, just aim to keep it into the wind. Continue the glide, keeping the nose of the model pointing slightly down all the time and if the machine is coming in steadily and not too fast, it is probably safer not to try to 'flare out' for the landing by using some up elevator. If the model is descending rather fast we must be prepared to feed in a little (I do mean a little) up elevator to slow the model down for the landing, but be careful not to allow the model to start climbing again with the risk of a stall. Judging when, and how much, up elevator to apply for 'rounding out' the model for a gentle touch down can only come with experience, but is something to look forward to.

Many importers and manufacturers now market "badge engineered" radio control equipment i.e. the outfits are produced by a different manufacturer but the supplier's name label, often in conjunction with the original manufacturer's name, is affixed to the goods.

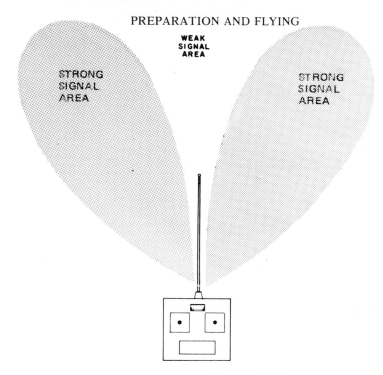

ANTENNA RADIATION PATTERN

Above, radiation pattern as given in Kraft instruction booklet supplied with typical equipment as at right, for 4 function control.

So there we are, on the ground safely again—at least if we have been lucky, and the most difficult part is over. Do remember to switch off both the transmitter and the receiver before taking a break to analyse constructively exactly what happened. Best of all, make a few written notes, also make the necessary adjustments to the rudder and elevator so that we can centralise the transmitter trims again. (I have assumed that the trims were not changed on the transmitter during the glide—this can be sorted out during later

flights). Think carefully when adjusting the clevises to the rudder and elevator horns it is all too easy to turn them in the wrong direction unless you are concentrating

When you have recovered, prepare to fly again, but check the model over thoroughly again to make sure all is working correctly and that the flying surfaces are on straight.

Before considering a few more of the pitfalls the unwary drop into, it may be worth making a précis of the foregoing sequence—write down on a card and ask your helper to check you through it.

1. Check flying area and weather.
2. Start and set engine.
3. Switch on and check radio.
4. Launch into wind and climb upwind.
5. Turn 180° to downwind.
6. As model travels downwind past you, turn the machine upwind again.
7. Gain height with left hand circuits.
8. When engine cuts continue left hand circuits.
9. Make final turn into wind with plenty of height.
10. Do not over correct elevator on landing—into wind.
11. Switch off and make trim adjustments.
12. Check model before next flight.

When you have been flying radio control models for some years, it is difficult to recall the problems experienced during the 'fledgling' stage. It is rather like riding a bicycle, once you have mastered the machine, it is difficult to remember why you could not ride it before. However, here are a few problems that are fairly common.

Although you are busy 'feeding' information to the model there is no passing back of information from the model to the transmitter. You must rely purely on visual acknowledgement of any control introduced. The sound of the engine can provide some useful information as to the attitude of the model. For example the lack of sound when the motor stops is obvious . . . equally, any speed up in the note of the engine, indicates that a dive has developed but it is better if you can learn to ignore sound as much as

A one sixth scale model of the Albatros C1 designed by the author for the BBC television series "Wings".

possible. One reason for this is that sound travels relatively slowly and therefore there is a delay between what happens to the aircraft and resultant sound reaching the pilot. Another reason for ignoring sounds is that later, when you are a confident pilot, you may be flying with four or five other models and then you will not be able to hear your own engine. Even the visual contact with the model causes a time lag; the model turns, the brain notes this and passes a message to this effect to the hands and corrective action is taken. There is now a further time lag before the model starts to react to the new position of the control surface. The result of these delays and time lags is that when action is taken it often has to be more drastic than one would wish and overcontrolling occurs.

Anticipation is the only way of overcoming this problem and, after a few dozen flights, this starts to become automatic. It can be compared with driving a car around a corner, initially one tends to turn only when the car reaches the corner and one has to put on a full lock. With experience, you anticipate the corner and start turning in good time making it into a gradual and flowing motion.

Orientation, knowing whether the model is coming towards you or going away from you, must be another of the main causes of trouble for the learner. Knowing instinctively that it is coming towards you, and which way to operate the rudder is a most important part of the game. Imagine yourself in the cockpit of the model and then the transmitter will always be relative to the model. To think in terms of 'left rudder is right rudder' etc., when the model is coming towards you, or to attempt to fly the model by looking over your shoulder at it (the latter to keep yourself in the same relative position to the model) are bad habits to be avoided. It is important when flying the model never to take your eyes from it, even a second or two looking at something else may induce problems in deciding the attitude of the model when you refocus on it. The **'Pronto'** is not too bad for ascertaining its attitude in the air. Some low wing models without dihedral can be most difficult to determine with regard to direction and attitude and can even present difficulty in deciding whether it is upright or inverted. Avoid going too high or too far away, the smaller the model appears the greater the difficulty is determining what corrective action is required. I would like a pound for everytime I have suggested (bawled out!) to a trainee to keep the model upwind at all costs. Even in a light wind it is amazing how much faster over the ground the model travels downwind compared with upwind. (A model with an air speed of 20 m.p.h. flying in a wind of 8 m.p.h. will travel over twice as fast down-wind as upwind). **KEEP UPWIND!**

Since the most dangerous times during a flight are launching and landing, and because there is no way to avoid them (it just ain't possible!) it is important for the beginner to experience and practise these two situations as much as possible.

One piece of trimming we still have to do is trimming the model for the glide which must be done after the initial test flights. We may find that when the engine cuts, the 'Pronto' does not require any substantial change of rudder or elevator trim but the chances are that some adjustments will be required. It is not possible to have perfectly constant trim positions for all conditions from full throttle to engine off. The amount of engine side thrust and down thrust should, ideally, be varied to counteract the varied engine torque and thrust through the full range of engine speeds. This, however, is impractical and we have to make small adjustments to the rudder and elevator trim controls instead.

What we are aiming to do at this stage is to eliminate any gross changes of trim on the transition from power flight to the glide and keep well within the range of transmitter trims.

Let us consider the possibilities:—

(a) From straight and level powered flight the model turns left on glide. Correction: Less engine side thrust required.

(b) From straight and level powered flight the model climbs on glide. Correction: Less engine down thrust required.

Obviously the reverse of these effects also apply. Once the adjustments to engine thrust lines have been made, as described in Chapter 7, rudder and elevator adjustments must also be made for correct flight under power. With a reduction of engine side thrust, the model is obviously now going to tend to turn to the left under power and some right rudder must be added to counteract this. Equally with down thrust reduced, more down elevator must be introduced. Carry out all adjustments a little at a time.

Finally a couple of quickies—I have suggested left hand circuits because these are slightly safer; the right engine thrust acts as upthrust when the model banks steeply to the left, lessening the risk of the nose dropping and the model getting into a spiral dive. I have not included any instructions for taking off a model from the ground, as opposed to hand launching, because many modellers do not have a suitable area of smooth grass or tarmac for this purpose.

CHAPTER NINE

CONCLUSIONS, PROBLEMS AND FAULTS

HAVING SPENT many happy hours at flying fields both watching and, I hope, helping some of the budding R/C fliers it is natural that one comes to some personal conclusions. I also carried out a number of experiments with modellers learning to fly and these were some of my findings.

Firstly, the method of learning to fly, my order or recommendation would be:—

(1) With the 'buddy box' system and an experienced pilot on the master transmitter. Using the linked system of transmitters avoids the undignified snatching away of the transmitter, sometimes unnecessarily and sometimes too late, from the pupil. It helps to promote confidence in the pupil and it is easy to demonstrate particular flying faults and problems. On occasions it does require some deft footwork on the part of the instructor, as the model flies overhead and the pupil rapidly turns to follow the model, but this is infinitely preferable to having one's eyes poked out by the pupil suddenly swinging around with the transmitter aerial scything through the air. The 'slave' transmitter does not need to have the transmitter extended, of course.

(2) With the pupil using a standard transmitter and an experienced and

The "buddy box" system of training is ideal for the beginner. It is not essential to have the aerial extended on the pupil's transmitter.

understanding flyer standing by to give advice and physical assistance when required. Modellers' characters vary as much as do the flying characteristics of different models and some will call for assistance at the first signs of anything apparently unusual happening. Others will only call out when it is lost. Even the most experienced R/C pilot can do little if he is presented with a transmitter when the model is in a vertical nose dive some ten feet from the ground and in a vaguely defined direction. The instructor must be able to assess the character of his pupil as well as his potential.

(3) A modeller and assistant — with no previous flying experience of any type — learning to fly without any help except from reading this book and other articles. I must be honest and say that, for the true 'loner' I do not think that the chances of success (without a lot of setbacks requiring considerable dedication to accept and overcome) can be greater than about 20 per cent. Assuming that the model is perfectly built and trimmed — unusual in itself for a first model — there are still the problems of getting the model into the air, keeping it within a reasonable distance of the transmitter and getting it safely on to the ground again. To achieve all this you need a certain amount of luck and a lot of fortitude. I am afraid a lot of would-be converts to our hobby give up, without success, for lack of practical help. The moral is obvious, even if it entails a long journey, or delays in flying, do try to get help before undertaking those first flights. Your model and radio equipment represent a considerable investment of cash and it would seem bad economics, at the least, to risk it all for the lack of a little assistance and advice. I hope that my depressing conclusions may prove to be unfounded and I would be interested to hear experiences of any readers who have 'done their own thing.'

Common Problems and Faults

I said earlier that many of the problems encountered by trainee R/C pilots were common ones and here is a summary of the most frequent.

On the ground:

(a) Insufficient preparation of the model and equipment. The model must balance on, or slightly in front of the designed position. A 'nearly' correct balance point (usually about one inch behind the recommended position) is not good enough and will probably result in disaster.

(b) Incorrect setting of the engine. Many modellers adjust the needle valve on their engines too rapidly, it takes a little time for the engines to respond to a change of needle position. Make adjustments slowly and in small increments, hold the model with the nose vertical before contemplating launching — if the revs drop, or the engine tends to cut, the needle valve must be opened up a little even if the engine tends to seem a little rich on the ground. The engine will probably lean out in the air and even if it continues to run a little on the rich side this is still preferable to having the engine cutting suddenly at an inconvenient time.

(c) For training models I still prefer hand launches to take offs for the learner. With a take off, the trainee has to try to keep the model straight on

Two views of the "Craftsman", the author's slender fuselage design which can be rudder only or used with additional strip elevator. Plans on two following pages.

the ground and judge when to apply a little up elevator to lift the model off. He more often than not finishes up hauling the model off too soon, out of wind and with one wing down — slow air speed, in a turn and near to the ground, which spells trouble. Admittedly, though, a good launch is required.

Ex-free flight modellers tend to be gentle and do not give enough push, non-aeromodellers tend to be the opposite and assume that the model will have a better chance if it is launched, a-la-javelin, towards the sky.

(d) With the model well launched, and reasonably trimmed, very little rudder or elevator correction should be necessary — small movements on the transmitter sticks only, please, to avoid over-correction.

(e) When the model is at a safe height, try to be bold and test the model for stalling with various engine settings and in turns. It is safer to find out what happens to the model with plenty of height for recovery than close to the ground on a landing approach.

(f) If you are still suffering from disorientation — and most learners will — go back to static training, hanging the model up in the living room, etc., as described in an earlier part.

(g) Do not be tempted to fly for too long a period on early flights, about five minutes of concentration is long enough. After that you can become confused, the problems of disorientation increase and reaction times also increase.

(h) The first action after encountering trouble with the model should always be to close the throttle. This will reduce the speed of the model and give you more time to think about what is happening. If the model is a long way away from the transmitter, and at a low altitude, first get the model on a level keel, aimed back towards you and then open the throttle gently.

(i) I have frequently watched modellers struggling to control a model that is way down wind, at height, and getting further away. Once you have the model pointing back towards you, put in some down elevator so that it goes into a shallow, but positive dive. Keep about 2/3rds power on and keep tracking towards you — this is the quickest way of getting back from a downwind position. Of course, you should not have been there in the first place!

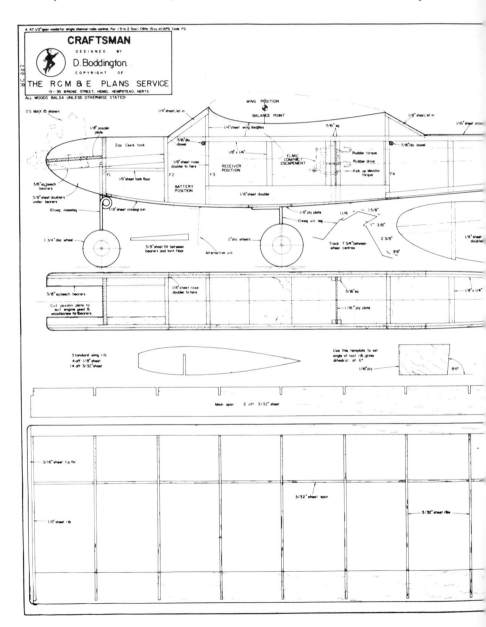

(j) It is always preferable to carry out your circuit and landing with the engine still running — a further reason for limiting your flight time. In this way you are able to go round again should you make a mess of your approach. By arranging your throttle so that the engine will cut, when full

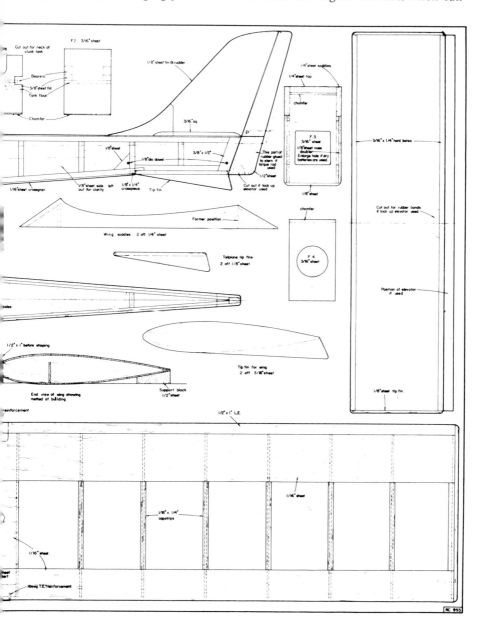

low trim is selected on the transmitter, the engine can be stopped when you are certain of your landing approach.

(k) Do keep to a planned landing circuit and give yourself plenty of time for a straight final approach, limited to minor adjustments. For some reason learners seem to become mesmerised by the model during the final part of landing, allowing the model to drift where it will. By all means avoid making large corrections but the model must still be guided into wind and given a slight flair out before touch down.

(l) One of the most difficult situations the learner can find himself in is to make the final approach, without engine, too high, flying over the landing area at about 30 ft. up. If the field is large, and you have plenty of area ahead, carry on and land straight ahead. With limited space available, you have to make a different decision. In no wind conditions there is no problem as the model can be turned up through 90 deg. or 180 deg. and landed but, with a prevailing wind, you must carry out a small 360 deg. turn and land. This is a difficult operation because you have to turn tightly near the ground (keep the turn going all the time — there is a temptation to ease off the rudder half way through the turn) and you must not let the nose of the model drop or rise too much in the turn. The remedy is to avoid getting into this position by judging your circuit more carefully, but this does take experience of differing wind conditions.

(m) The more difficult operation in all forms of flying is to get the aircraft back on to the ground safely. As we cannot avoid this problem it is better to practise it and become proficient at it.

Novel composite R/C model comprises a 90 inch wing span parasol "Mighty Barnstormer" with small 1.5 cc. powered, "Twinkle" models fitted to the underside of the wings. Three function radio equipment is used in the "parasite" models and five function in the "mother" aircraft —the fifth function being used for releasing the small models in the air.

CHAPTER TEN

FUTURE MODELS

HOW LONG a modeller takes to become proficient at the basic skills of flying a radio control model varies enormously from person to person. Some take to it like the proverbial duck to water but, for others, it is a fairly prolonged, and at times anguished, period. Once these basic flying skills have been mastered, the modeller can reliably take off, or control the model from a hand launch, fly around in a positive manner and land safely back. This is the time that he will be contemplating the next challenge.

To most enthusiasts this will mean a model that is more aerobatic and faster than the basic trainer of the 'Pronto' type. Perhaps some of you will be contemplating branching out to specialised aspects of the hobby such as scale or pylon racing. To jump straight from a basic trainer to serious involvement in one of these departments is, in my opinion, too great a leap. It is much better to progress gradually, through purpose designed sports training models, and build up to a full confidence in flying before going on to more demanding models. The **'Sky Rider'** and **'Ghost Rider 50'** are intended as a suitable second step towards the goal of full flying proficiency.

Design criteria for these models included a reasonable degree of positive stability so that, although you must control them to a greater degree than the 'Pronto' it still allows a certain amount of relaxation at the transmitter. With ailerons fitted, it will give you an opportunity to co-ordinate all control functions i.e. elevator, rudder, ailerons and engine throttle, a task that requires a model that is reasonably easy to fly and without vices. The **Sky Rider** and **GR50** were also designed to have a medium wing loading to allow the model to be flown at sensible speeds on the landing approach without suddenly dropping a wing or falling out of the sky. By using a shoulder wing configuration, as compared with a low wing design, a greater degree of lateral stability is obtained and it also allows the model to be hand launched more easily. Tricycle undercarriages are incorporated for the benefit of those fortunate enough to have a decent take off strip. If you fly from a field with grass that is not too rough and you would still like to have a try at take offs, I would suggest using a longer nose wheel leg and main undercarriage to give plenty of clearance for the propeller on tufts of grass, and to use a size larger in wheels. The great virtue of a tricycle undercarriage during take off is that it helps to make the model 'track' a lot straighter than the two wheel variety. This can be of considerable assistance during the period when you are getting used to the change of operating the rudder on the left hand transmitter stick and the ailerons from the right hand stick (when ailerons are not used the rudder is controlled from the right hand stick). Only small rudder movements will be needed for direction adjustments during the take off run, indeed if the model is launched directly into wind, and the wheels are carefully aligned to track straight, no correction may be required. Steerable nose-wheels are not shown on the drawings. This is a refinement that allows steerable taxying, but is not essential for take off and landing, and is therefore omitted in the cause of simplicity.

The wings are secured to the fuselages by the 'old fashioned' method of rubber bands — not such a neat method as the peg and bolt system used on many multi-aerobatic models but very much more forgiving when the model is inadvertently landed wing tip first. Strip ailerons are incorporated on the **'Sky Rider'** and **'Pronto'** in preference to outboard type, again for reasons of simplicity but the linkage from the aileron servo suggested is built into the wing and connects to a horn in the centre of the strip ailerons.

The centre horn position on the strip aileron of the **'Sky Rider'** assists in eliminating aileron 'flutter' when the model is flying at high speed. Flutter occurs when the air flow and pressure on the aileron is sufficient to overcome the force applied by the servo and linkage; the aileron is pushed back and, together with turbulence around the aileron and hinge line, causes the ailerons to develop a high frequency oscillation. Top hinged strip ailerons, using Kwik Cote or Solarfilm full span hinges tend to suffer less from this problem of 'flutter' as it reduces the turbulence caused by a gap at the hinge line.

For a 'second step' training model the **'Sky Rider'** is adequately powered by a .40 cu. in. R/C engine, this will give sufficient power for basic aerobatics

Advanced trainer, such as the "Sky Rider" shown here, is the next step from the "Pronto." With a wing span of 63 inches the "Sky Rider" is suitable for 3-4 function radio and .40-.60 cu. ins. engine.

"Sky Rider 63" Aerobatic trainer. Ideal follow up to the "Pronto."

and pull the model around fast enough for most modellers at this stage. Alternatively, the **'Ghost Rider 50'** will take the same engine you used in the **'Pronto'.** Remember that excessive power can get you into trouble as well as getting you out of trouble at times. It is a little like a high powered car, once you know how to handle all of the power available, it can assist to obtain maximum manoeuvrability, but in the hands of the novice, this extra power will cause difficulties.

Some modellers may be hoping to progress onto larger models, of one type or another, and wish to purchase a .60 cu. in. engine at this stage. Provided one is prepared to limit the power of a larger engine initially it should not prove to be an embarrassment. A simple method of restricting the thrust from the engine is to fit the propeller on backwards, alternatively set the motor servo movement so that it will not open the carburettor fully. Needless to say if you are looking for something less than full power there is no point in using anything other than a 'straight' fuel mix. Large capacity engines (.30 cu. in. upwards, except for racing engines) will perform quite happily on un-nitrated fuel although some of the smaller engines prefer a fuel with a moderate nitro methane content.

The author posing with his model Sopwith Pup in front of the full size aircraft at the Shuttleworth Collection, Old Warden, Beds.

Flying an Aerobatic Trainer

Test flying an aerobatic training model. such as the **'Ghost Rider 50'** or **'Sky Rider'** is slightly different to the **'Pronto'**. I am assuming, for convenience sake, that ailerons were not fitted to the previous trainer and this will be your first experience with them. A slight to moderate wind will not present too much of a problem on initial flights but test gliding, because of the models wing loading and flying speed, is completely out.

Hand launching is not difficult, due to the shoulder wing layout, but it needs to be launched reasonably fast and level. I am inclined to the opinion that a hand launch is preferable to a take off for someone without previous experience on this type of model. The reason behind this thinking is that rudder control is now on the left hand stick (previously, it was on the right hand stick) and rudder control may be required during a take off. From a hand launch the rudder need not be touched until the model is at a safe height, when rudder control can be experimented with, and its use gradually familiarised. Further homework, by operating the controls at home to become completely experienced with the use of all four control axis, will also pay off when you come to the first flight.

Aileron control differs from rudder control in a number of ways. You will find that the model banks much more quickly than with the use of rudder control — no waiting for the model to yaw before it banks and turns. On the other hand, to achieve a turn, banking must be applied followed by up elevator to pull the model round. Initially you may find you are over controlling, with over corrections on the aileron; try to keep your movements smooth and proportional rather than quick stabs of the stick. Apart from the additional speed, you will also notice that the model will tend to fly in the direction it is positioned until further correction is made. It has not the same degree of inherent stability as the 'Pronto' and must be controlled for most of its flight, although it is not vicious in any respect. The important part to remember when flying an aerobatic model of this type is that you must be positive in your approach; never let the model wander around the sky where it will, position it where you want it to go. What is required is firm but gentle control, a quality my R.A.F. instructor used to call 'the touch of a midwife.' On the first flight keep the engine at full bore until you have reached a safe height of 200 ft. or so before testing out the slow speed characteristics and retrimming. Naturally, even if you feel fairly proficient at flying a basic training model, it is preferable to hand over the model to a qualified pilot for initial flight testing and if you can then graduate by the use of a 'buddy box' — so much the better. Assuming that the model has the fin and rudder correctly aligned, any turning tendencies should be cured by adjustments to the ailerons, initially on the up going aileron but, if a couple of turns on the clevis doesn't cure the bank, then on both ailerons. Elevator adjustments and/or engine down thrust changes should be made as previously described but remember that the glide will be that much faster. Do persevere with the trimming out of the model until you have it as near perfect over the full speed range as possible. Trimming out also involves the engine control, aim for a minimum safe idling speed with the throttle stick fully back but with the trim lever fully forward. The final movement of the trim lever should then cut the engine completely.

Taking off a model from a smooth surface is very simple providing you follow three basic principles.

1. The undercarriage is set up to track straight, adjust the nosewheel and main wheels until the model runs straight.

2. The model is released directly into wind.

3. You do not 'haul' the model off the ground before ample flying speed is reached.

If these three principles are observed the chances are that no correction will be required during the take off run but, should the model track to one side or the other, correct with rudder releasing as soon as the original heading is recovered. Never allow a take off swing to develop before recovery action is taken, try to anticipate the model's action so that only a small correction is required. Any violent swing due to over correction, should result in an aborted take off — chop the throttle otherwise you are likely to find yourself airborne, out of wind, with one wing too low and short of airspeed too. The actual lift off should be achieved by the application of gradual and slight up elevator so that a gentle climb out is obtained and not a sudden leap into the air.

Aerobatics

When you are completely happy flying the aerobatic trainer at all speeds, heights and attitudes the control movement of the ailerons, rudder and elevator can be increased to extend your aerobatic vocabulary. The **'GR50'** and **'Sky Rider'** models are designed as aerobatic trainers so do not expect them to perform the full aerobatic schedule with the same accuracy as a sophisticated and specialised aerobatic model. They will perform nearly all of the individual schedule manoeuvres but the rolls will not be quite as axial and you may be running out of 'steam' on some of the vertical manoeuvres.

Before contemplating any aerobatics do make sure you have plenty of wing retaining bands on, at least eight heavy rubber bands, and before going into any specific manoeuvre take a quick look around to make sure there are no other models flying in the area that you might collide with.

LOOP. Probably the simplest of all aerobatics. Enter the loop at full power and with the wings level pulling in about ¾ of up elevator and, as the model goes past the inverted position, reduce power to half and gradually apply full up elevator as the model is coming through the vertical position. You may have to make some aileron correction to keep the wings level through the loop although carrying out the manoeuvre directly into wind will help in this respect. To carry out consecutive loops full power can be maintained but elevator adjustments will be necessary, easing off the up elevator as the model pulls out into wind, to avoid drifting back with the prevailing wind.

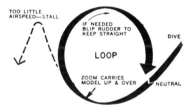

SLOW ROLL. Most models will roll faster in one direction, normally to the right, than the other so experiment with your model to check roll rates. Initially you should practise slow, axial, rolls at a good height to give yourself plenty of room to pull through (a half loop from the inverted position) should you get into difficulties. There are sound reasons for slow rolling a model in a down wind direction for competition work but, in a strong wind, too much ground will be covered for training purposes and I would suggest practising them into the wind. Commence the roll with full power, and the nose slightly high, apply full aileron movement and, when the model has rolled past the vertical and is approaching the inverted position, feed in enough down elevator to keep the nose of the model slightly above the horizon. As the model passes the inverted position towards the vertical ease off the down elevator and, during the final quarter of the roll, it may be necessary to feed in a small amount of up elevator. There are two common faults that beginners make when attempting rolls for the first time. One is to let the nose drop too low

"Ghost Rider 38," one of the Author's most recent designs, specifically created for rudder/elevator control.

during the inverted section of the roll, if this happens, close the throttle and pull through by applying up elevator — hence the need for plenty of height. The second fault is a tendency to take off aileron as the model is half way through the roll — keep the aileron stick over all the time.

BARREL ROLL. This can be described as a corkscrew loop as it is a com-

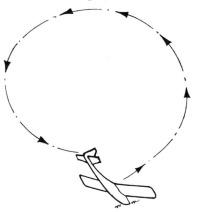

The path of a barrel roll.

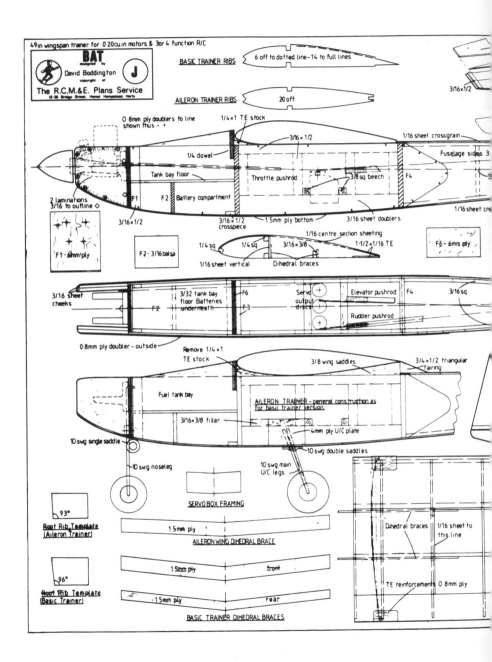

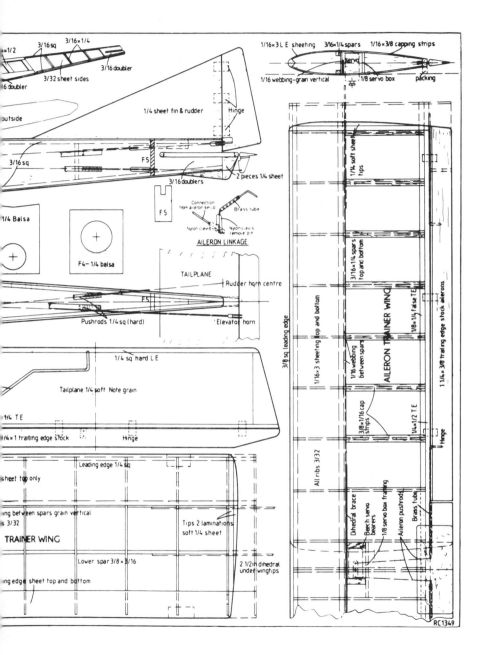

RC 1349

"Tyro", designed originally for rudder only, often converted with elevator control, always a very popular design, plans on preceding pages.

bination of a loop and roll. Initially you will find it easier to commence the manoeuvre by going into a shallow dive banking in the opposite direction to that of the barrel roll. Start to pull in up elevator and, at the same time, aileron and the model will climb and roll. Keep the roll going and the up elevator — it may need easing off a little over the top and increasing slightly as the model pulls out. A good barrel roll should maintain positive 'G' all the way round whereas with the slow roll you would, if you were sitting in the cockpit, be hanging by your harness straps during the inverted stage.

STALL TURN. You will see few true stall turns at the average club flying fields unless they have some good aerobatic pilots. The idea of a stall turn is to climb the model vertically and hold it in that position until the stall is virtually reached before applying rudder to bring the nose through a full 180° and the model descends in the vertical position. Most flyers operate the rudder at too high a speed and the result is more of a tight wing over rather than a stall turn. Commence the stall by diving to build up some extra speed, pull up with the wings level, until the model is vertical. The extra speed gives us more time to make adjustments to get the model vertical and hold it there. Cut the throttle and when the model has decelerated to about stalling speed (only experience will tell you this), then apply full rudder. As with the slow roll you will probably find that your model will turn better in one direction than the other. With the model now in the vertically down position ease on up elevator and, as it rounds out, apply power. The stall turn is a difficult manoeuvre to do consistently and requires much practice.

INVERTED FLIGHT. Because aerobatic trainers are usually designed with a certain degree of longitudinal stability, i.e. the wing is at a greater positive incidence than the tailplane, you will find that it requires a certain amount of down elevator held in during inverted flight to prevent the nose dropping. The tendency for the nose to drop is increased during an inverted turn. The inverted position is easiest to attain by performing a half roll and taking off the aileron when the inverted is reached. Aileron control remains the same i.e. left aileron stick on the transmitter will turn the model to the left, but elevator is reversed and to make the model climb down elevator must be applied. Theoretically you should be able to fly a model round inverted as easily as in the upright position but it will be some time before you are able to do a low inverted fly past in a relaxed manner.

OUTSIDE LOOP or **BUNT.** This is the opposite of a normal inside loop so, instead of applying up elevator you put in down elevator. Before attempting a full inverted loop try a half bunt from the inverted position. Fly along straight and level, in the inverted position, and push in nearly full down elevator until the model describes a half circle to the upright level position. For a full bunt the entry is from normal straight and level flight but with low power, as the model tucks under to the inverted position start applying power to keep the speed up for the second half of the manoeuvre. Avoid the temptation of easing off the down elevator as the model goes past the vertical in the dive — it can be slightly terrifying but you are likely to finish up with more panic if you abandon the manoeuvre at this stage. As with most manoeuvres small corrections of ailerons will probably be required at some point and the accuracy and consistency of the manoeuvres represent the difference between a 'fly for fun' pilot and a competition modeller.

SPINS. With limited rudder and elevator movements you may find it difficult to get the model into a spin. I therefore suggest that spinning is only practised when these movements have been increased. To enter a spin climb the model (plenty of height) and throttle back the engine, pull the nose well up so that the model is at least at 60° by the time stalling speed is reached. At this point give simultaneously full up and full rudder, the model should then flick over and start autorotating (revolving round its own axis) in a nose down attitude. To get out of the spin it should only be necessary to centralise the controls and gradually ease back on the elevator as the speed builds up.

Large models are becoming increasingly popular and the "Mighty Mannock" 80 inch wing span model by the author is easy to fly and can be powered by engines from .60 to .90 cu. ins. capacity.

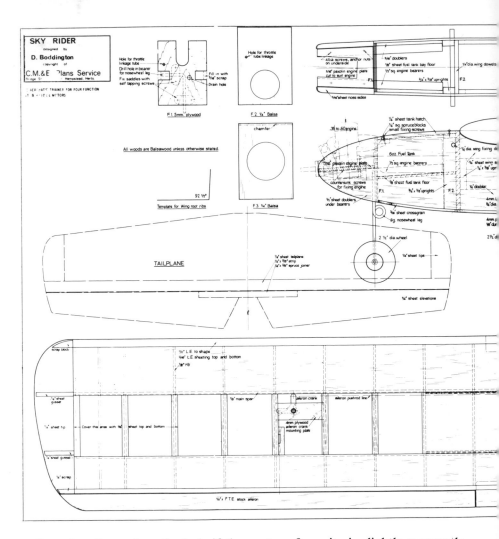

Occasionally, and particularly if the centre of gravity is slightly rearwards, the model may tend to flatten in the spin with the result that the model does not stop spinning when controls are neutralised. In this case give full down elevator and, as the nose drops and the speed increases, apply opposite rudder to reduce the rotation. Never apply opposite rudder before down elevator as this will probably result in the model flicking from a spin in one direction to a spin in the opposite direction. Should the application of down elevator in no way reduce the flattened spin attitude then the only remaining action is to apply down elevator and full engine together to try to 'rock' the model to a

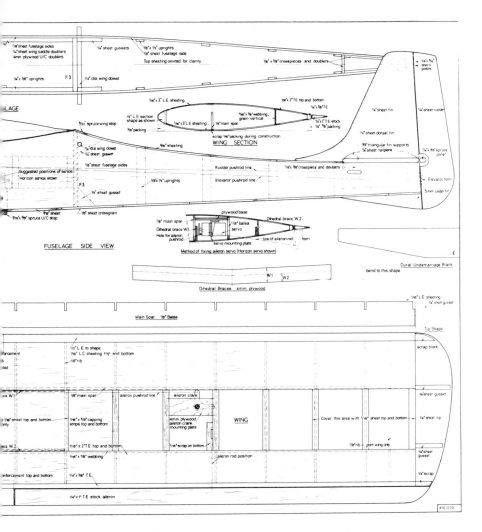

nose down attitude if necessary by 'pumping' the two functions, up and low throttle, down and full throttle. When this type of action is required you can be certain that the model is tail heavy.

Inverted spins are approached in a similar manner to a normal spin but from the inverted position and by applying full down elevator and rudder. Recovery too is similar but up elevator is introduced if the spin does not cease with the centralising of the sticks.

COMBINATION MANOEUVRES. Manoeuvres such as Cuban Eight and

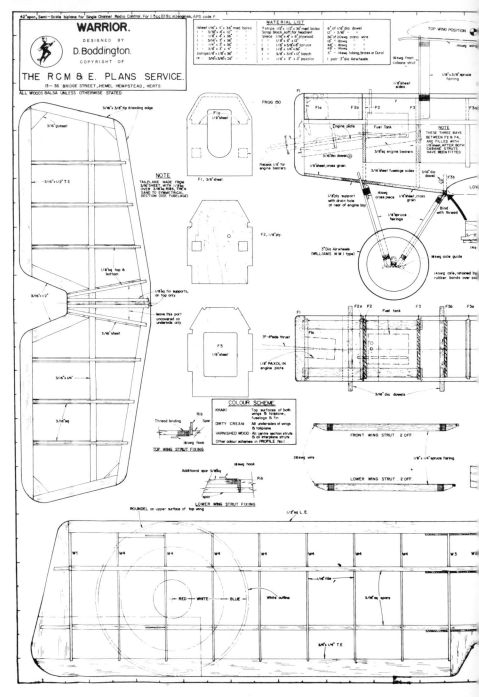

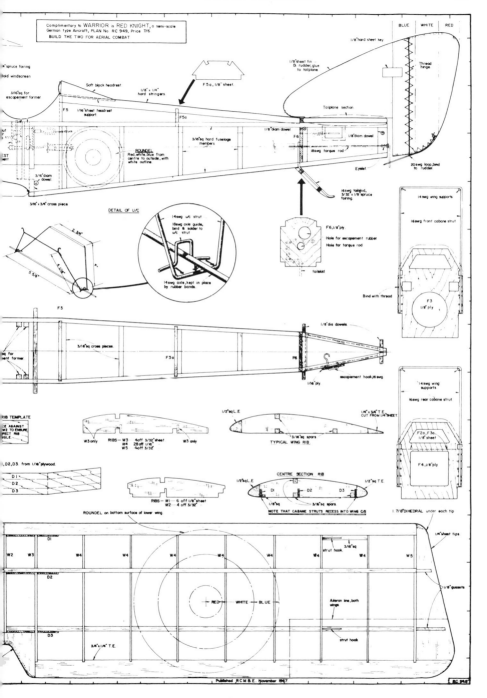

Complimentary to WARRIOR is RED KNIGHT, a semi-scale
German type Aircraft, PLAN No RC 949, Price 7/6
BUILD THE TWO FOR AERIAL COMBAT

Published R.C.M.& E. November 1967

RC 949

"Red Arrow" low wing design for full multi control and engines from .19 to .35.
Fully aerobatic but with sports appearance. Plans on following pages.

Reversals are a combination of the basic manoeuvres and can be practised when the basics are learnt.

KNIFE EDGE. Knife edge flying is when the model is on its side i.e. with the wings vertical and maintains this attitude in forward level flight. To achieve it the model must be rolled through 90° and, as it reaches the vertical wing position and the nose high, top rudder must be applied and the aileron centralised. The top rudder is then acting as 'up elevator' to hold the nose of the model up and for the lift required for flight to be obtained from the fuselage. You may be able to achieve a limited degree of knife edge flying, but it really needs a specialised aerobatic model for sustained knife edging and, even then, it is difficult to hold.

FLICK MANOEUVRES. Flick manoeuvres are really horizontal spins and are entered from the upright or inverted position. With the nose held slightly high let the speed of the model drop off, to a point, which can only be determined by experiment, before applying full rudder and elevator. Large rudder and elevator movements and a slightly rearward centre of gravity are required for these manoeuvres and, with practice, the degree of rotation (i.e. one complete flick or 1½ flicks) can be controlled by releasing the controls at the correct time.

There are a few more specialised aerobatic manoeuvres such as Llomchervak's and Avalanches, mainly based on flick, or stalled, conditions but the ones described here should give plenty of food for thought and flying to attempt. In the meantime do not overlook your general flying, circuits should still be planned and landings by now should be 'on the spot' and fully con-

Ailerons approx.
neutral.

Top elevator

Nose high.

Knife edge flight.

Lift created
mainly from
the fuselage.

trolled. Even if you have no intentions of progressing to a fully fledged competition aerobatic model it is advisable to attempt all forms of aerobatics, you will have far more confidence in being able to extricate any future model from 'unusual' positions.

Author with his WW1 semi-scale
biplane "Warrior", plans on two
preceding pages.

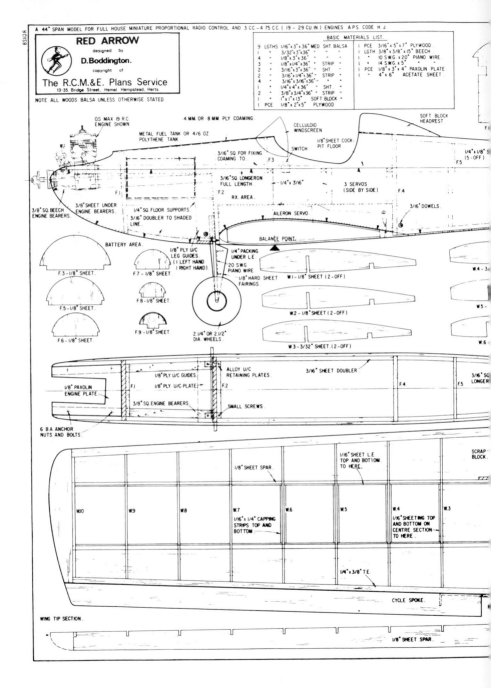

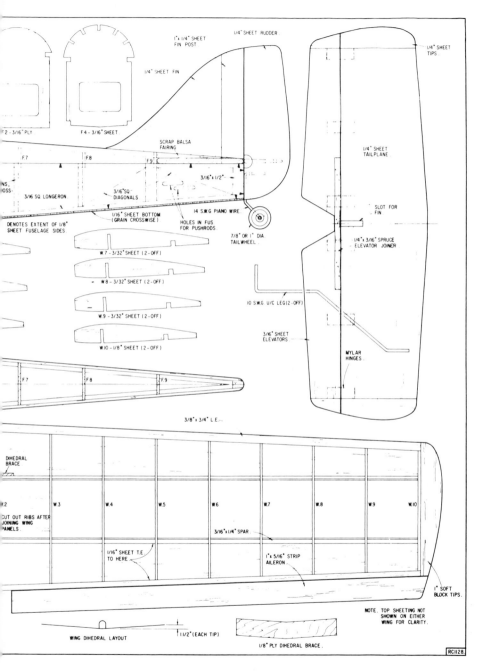

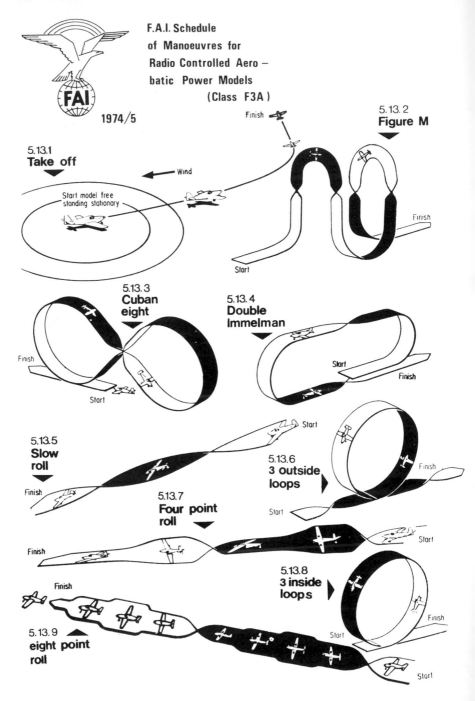

F.A.I. Schedule
of Manoeuvres for
Radio Controlled Aero —
batic Power Models
(Class F3A)

1974/5

5.13.1
Take off

Wind

Start model free
standing stationary

Finish

5.13.2
Figure M

Finish

Start

5.13.3
Cuban eight

Finish

Start

5.13.4
Double Immelman

Start

Finish

5.13.5
Slow roll

Finish

5.13.6
3 outside loops

Start

Finish

Start

5.13.7
Four point roll

Finish

Start

5.13.8
3 inside loops

Start

Finish

5.13.9
eight point roll

Finish

Start

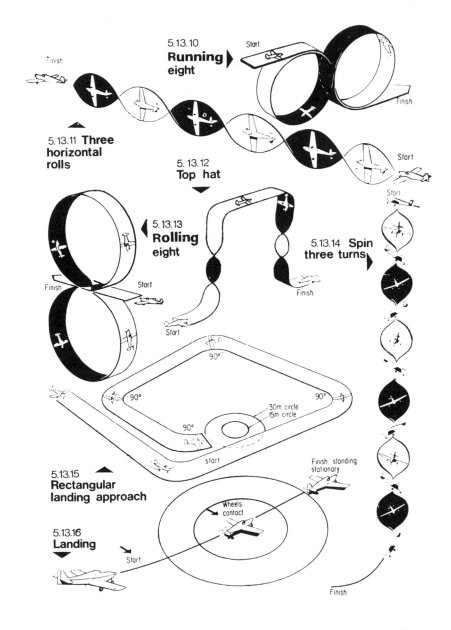

Finish

5.13.10 **Running eight** ▶

Start

Finish

▲ 5.13.11 **Three horizontal rolls**

5.13.12 **Top hat**

Start

◀ 5.13.13 **Rolling eight**

5.13.14 **Spin three turns** ▶

Start

Finish

Start

Finish

Start

Start

90°

90°

90°

90°

30m. circle
15m. circle

start

Finish standing stationary

5.13.15 ▲ **Rectangular landing approach**

Wheels contact

5.13.16 **Landing**

Start

Finish

What Next?

So, with all the basic skills of building and flying radio control models learnt, where do we go from here? There are so many avenues to explore, so many branches of the hobby to investigate that it is difficult to give you an idea of all the aspects of radio control aircraft. Indeed, it is no function of this book to explain to you all of the models you can go on to build and fly. Just to give you a glimpse of some of the possibilities for your future delights, however, consider some of these possibilities:—

(1) Gliders and Sailplanes — For slope soaring or thermal soaring.

(2) Pylon Racing — Three classes for .049 cu. in. engines to .40 cu. in. engines, for these miniature replicas of full size racing aircraft.

(3) Aerobatics — To many this, the challenge of pure aerobatics, is the main aim of the hobby. Dedication and practice is the only way to the top of aerobatic competitions.

(4) Scale — Miniature full size aircraft, complete in every detail. From replicas of the earliest aircraft to copies of four engine bombers and even jet airliners, all of these are feasible.

(5) Float Planes and Flying Boats — There is a special thrill in taking off and landing a model on water. In winter you can also have tremendous fun flying models fitted with skis.

(6) Helicopters — One of the latest introductions to the hobby, for many years it was thought to be impossible. It is a particularly fascinating, and rewarding sport.

(7) Sports Models — Probably the great proportion of radio control modellers are perfectly happy flying sports models and always will be, a sufficiently diverse choice of model types and experiments to carry out keeping any modeller busy for the rest of his life.

Included in this book are small scale reproductions of some of my plans for sports and scale models. To date, I have designed more than a hundred model aircraft (and built most). Far from running out of new subjects I can never find sufficient time to draw and construct the many that are 'doodled' on the back of envelopes or are only in the mind. I hope this book may have kindled your interest sufficiently to get you started along the interesting path of radio control model aircraft. Once started the next steps are yours. I can only promise you that the hobby will give you as much as you are prepared to put into it and, in pursuing the hobby, you will meet as friendly and helpful a group of people as you are likely to come across anywhere — it is that sort of hobby!

To end on a serious note, **please,** whenever and wherever you are flying, **FLY SAFELY.** Do not forget that although you are not legally required to be licensed for radio control operation you would be very foolish to fly without adequate insurance cover. Do go along and join your nearest club or group, this will help you by putting you in touch with modellers most of whom will be only too willing to help you.